The Space of the Screen
in Contemporary French
and Francophone Fiction

american
university
studies

Series II
Romance Languages and Literature

Vol. 227

PETER LANG
New York • Washington, D.C./Baltimore • Bern
Frankfurt am Main • Berlin • Brussels • Vienna • Oxford

Donna Wilkerson-Barker

The Space of the Screen in Contemporary French and Francophone Fiction

PETER LANG
New York • Washington, D.C./Baltimore • Bern
Frankfurt am Main • Berlin • Brussels • Vienna • Oxford

Library of Congress Cataloging-in-Publication Data

Wilkerson-Barker, Donna.
The space of the screen in contemporary French
and francophone fiction / Donna Wilkerson-Barker.
p. cm. — (American university studies. Series II,
Romance languages and literature; v. 227)
Originally presented as the author's thesis (Ph.D.—University of
North Carolina at Chapel Hill, 1999) under the title:
Image technologies and literature.
Includes bibliographical references.
1. French fiction—20th century—History and criticism. 2. Visual perception
in literature. 3. Genet, Jean, 1910– —Criticism and interpretation.
4. Guibert, Hervé—Criticism and interpretation. 5. Bouraoui, Nina—
Criticism and interpretation. I. Title. II. American university studies.
Series II, Romance languages and literature; v. 227.
PQ673 .W53   843'.9109353—dc21   2002016249
ISBN 0-8204-5831-7
ISSN 0740-9257

Die Deutsche Bibliothek-CIP-Einheitsaufnahme

Wilkerson-Barker, Donna.
The space of the screen in contemporary French
and Francophone fiction / Donna Wilkerson-Barker.
–New York; Washington, D.C./Baltimore; Bern;
Frankfurt am Main; Berlin; Brussels; Vienna; Oxford: Lang.
(American university studies: Ser. 2,
Romance languages and literature; Vol. 227)
ISBN 0-8204-5831-7

The paper in this book meets the guidelines for permanence and durability
of the Committee on Production Guidelines for Book Longevity
of the Council of Library Resources.

© 2003 Peter Lang Publishing, Inc., New York
275 Seventh Avenue, 28th Floor, New York, NY 10001
www.peterlangusa.com

Printed in the United States of America

TABLE OF CONTENTS

ACKNOWLEDGMENTS

A slightly modified version of the section "Imperialism, Nationalism, and Interculturality in Technicolor" was previously published in *Word & Image* 18(1) 2002: 53–56. Reprinted by permission of the publisher. All rights reserved.

The sections "Spectral Images," "The Spectral Image and *Mon Valet et Moi*," and "The Disappearing Portrait of the Man in the Red Hat" were published in modified form in *Studies in Twentieth Century Literature* 19(2) 1995: 269–288. Reprinted by permission of the publisher. All rights reserved.

PROLOGUE | Bookspace in the Electronic Age

Alongside the numerous "disappearing acts" at the end of the millennium (e.g. the "end of ideology;" the "end of History;" the "death of the author;" and the "death of the subject"), the book too has seemingly reached its end. As the development of technology and its impact on social and cultural practices make themselves felt, "bookspace" is increasingly associated with a paradigm weighted down by its relationship to hegemonic cultural practices.[1] New media, namely cyberspace and virtual reality technologies, are often postulated in this scenario as sites for the "radicalization" not only of print culture and its tenets, but also of democracy and community.[2]

At the same time, however, the encroachment of other media forms such as television, video, and photography onto everyday life experience is altering the cultural terrain on another level, contributing to a confusion of boundaries between reality and the image and weakening our ability to decipher history and shared popular memory. In discussions of postmodern culture, this phenomenon is commonly referred to as the culture of the simulacrum. The collective loss of a unified cultural memory and history, elements which have been rendered ephemeral in the electronic age, has certainly had a significant impact on reading, writing, and the position of the book today as well.

Not surprisingly, the notion of literacy within the present historical conjuncture has shifted. The book, far from finding itself at the center of the processes that define literacy, must indeed come to grips with the fact that

> we inhabit a photocentric, aural, and televisual culture in which the proliferation of photographic and electronically produced images and sounds serves as a form of media catechism—perpetual pedagogy—through which individuals ritually encode and evaluate the engagements they make in the various discursive contexts of everyday life. This form of literacy understands media representations—whether photographs, television, print, film or other forms—as productive not merely of knowledge, but also of subjectivity. (McLaren and Hammer 106)

No longer seen, then, as a viable paradigm for effecting change in the world, writing has been demoted from meaningful social praxis, transformed as it were into just another marketable object in consumer culture. As Jenaro Talens explains, "to be known as a writer usually does not necessarily mean to be read but to appear on TV shows or to be quoted in newspapers, and the circulation of names and/or titles through the mass media has been substituted for the dialogic familiarity with texts" (2).

Given this momentous epistemological shift, this study is concerned to develop some perspectives on the space of literature within an era increasingly in need of a critical *media* literacy. What is the status of literature now when cyberspace and television are the preferred mediums not only for entertainment, but also for information? How has literature evolved in the face of "technoculture?" And is literature as social praxis even viable today when "[t]he model of consciousness based on the book as text paradigm—implying the unity, stability, and coherence of the subject—is...undermined" by cyberspace models which offer "different text forms (including intertextuality, multi-textuality, hybrids of all kinds) ...along with new notions of collective and interactive agency and new political possibilities" (Lankshear et al., 167)?

In the following chapters, through readings of the work of three French writers, Jean Genet (1910–1986), Hervé Guibert (1955–1991), and Nina Bouraoui (1967–), I seek to explore different ways in which the space of literature serves precisely as a form of "media literacy," helping readers to position themselves critically in the face of image culture. Significantly, in Genet, Guibert, and Bouraoui, narrators take on the status of media spectators as they draw on newspapers, film, video, photography, and television (forms I group together and refer to as the space of the screen throughout this study) to represent autobiographical or historical experiences. For example, Genet's *Pompes funèbres* (1947) uses newspapers and cinema to tell the story of the death and burial of his lover during World War II, and his play *Les Paravents* (1961) stages the Arab uprising against colonialism at the start of the Algerian War through an elaborate use of screens and images which, in a broad cultural sense, represent the surfaces of photography, film, or television. Hervé Guibert's narratives *L'Image fantôme* (1981), *Mon Valet et moi* (1991), and *L'Homme au chapeau rouge* (1992) describe, through the documentary lens of photography and video, the everyday life experiences of a photo-journalist, including his contraction of AIDS. Nina Bouraoui's *La Voyeuse interdite* (1991) relates the story of a young Algerian woman sequestered since the onset of puberty due to the constraints imposed on women living under Islamic fundamentalism in the wake of decolonization. In this text, the narrator's windowpane, which is simultaneously the locus and mediator of her story, functions like a photograph or television as it allows the young girl to simultaneously enact cultural memories and create an alternate reality.

These authors' texts, in their recognition of the space of the screen as a site for the production of multiple forms of knowledge and subjectivity, thus create the space of literature as a space which is consonant with the shifting dynamics of image culture introduced above. Yet, because writing and the simulacrum are thought to belong to different pragmatic and epistemological worlds, the former being associated with stable meaning and the latter with a radical interactiveness, the extent to which literary space functions as a space of critical reflection on and within image culture has remained undertheorized.

The works of Genet, Guibert, and Bouraoui articulate the interface between writing and the image by placing media spectatorship at the center of narrative. My analysis of literary space is thus informed by an approach which explores and preserves the ambivalence constitutive of spectatorship in postmodern image culture. For as Ella Shohat and Robert Stam have noted, "[i]f spectatorship is on the one level structured and determined, on another level it is open and polymorphous…. Spectatorship can become a liminal space of dreams and self-fashioning. Through its psychic chameleonism, ordinary social positions, as in carnival, are temporarily bracketed" (355). Genet's, Guibert's, and Bouraoui's presentation of image culture from a variety of cultural voices—voices which are, moreover, routinely muffled or cast in stereotypical images in dominant media representations (i.e., the voices of criminals, colonized peoples, women, and people with AIDS)—reveals both the imperious side of the media and its ludic, more adventurous side, a side which is ultimately paired by these writers with the act of writing and its connections to cultural alterity and death.

Chapter one synthesizes the debates concerning writing and the simulacrum in order to provide conceptual groundwork for subsequent discussion. My aim is to demonstrate that even while simulation culture actively subverts "bookspace" in the public sphere, literature nevertheless remains an exemplary site for the production of a critical space of reflection from within which media culture can be explored. It does this by placing media spectatorship (the screen) at the center of narrative processes, demonstrating the power of the screen to produce homogenous and normative identities, as well as its capacity to be used otherwise. To delineate the latter problematic, I concentrate specifically on the ambivalence of the image in relation to death, subjectivity, and the body in technoculture, leitmotifs that will resurface in each subsequent chapter.

Chapter two considers the repercussions of image technologies on nationalism, history, and death in Jean Genet's work. I begin with an analysis of the space of the screen as a space for the creation of new subjectivities and identities throughout Genet's artistic corpus from a broad perspective. Then, I move on to explore the space of the screen as a space of negotiation with national and personal history and identity in *Pompes funèbres* and *Les Paravents*. In these texts, Genet deploys dominant media as a means to concurrently critique a Eurocentric vision of history and to create a space for intercultural negotiation, one of whose primary manifestations is symbolic exchange with the dead and death. While criticism on Genet has underlined the use of the media in his novels, as well as his continual problematization of the interplay between reality and illusion, thus far critics have remained encapsulated by their view of Genet the anarchist and purveyor of evil. Consequently, attention is shifted away from Genet's presentation of the image itself and toward his desire, as a social outcast, to undermine bourgeois social morality. It will not be my intention to question the validity of such inquiries. Rather, by locating Genet's aesthetic in the technological imagination, I will argue that far from stemming strictly from his own marginalized position in society, it is Genet's deep understanding of the image in consumer culture and its effect on the conception of death and sociality that creates the fragmentary subjectivity, ambivalent politics, and simulacrum effect particular to his work.

Chapter three concentrates on the function of image technologies in *L'Homme au chapeau rouge*, *Mon Valet et moi*, and *L'Image fantôme* by Hervé Guibert. Functioning as closely as possible to an actual video camera, Guibert's writing is an example *par excellence* of writing-as-image. Approached primarily from the perspective of subjectivity and the hyperreal, we will see that Guibert's novels, while working in conjunction with the Baudrillardian notion of simulation, nevertheless complicate it through their resistant readings of image culture based in personal experience, death and suffering. Guibert's writing project, I suggest, models the (photographic/video) image to such an extent that his texts take on its defining characteristics, thereby rendering a corpus of texts which is at once highly experimental and ambiguous.

Chapter four focuses on the dematerialization of the body in technoculture as it pertains to the female subject in *La Voyeuse interdite* by Nina Bouraoui. Through the projection of her gaze onto her windowpane, which takes on the allure of the screen, the young female narrator of this story conjures up images of (Arab) women that are part of a familiar repertoire in Orientalist, western, and Islamic fundamentalist imaginaries. Finding herself effectively "trapped" by the symbolic and cultural positionings of her body within these registers, the young protagonist turns to anorexia as a means to sever body from mind, a scenario that echoes contemporary forms of female empowerment fostered by the media. Through an analysis of the figure of the anorectic in Bouraoui, then, we will focus closely on the position of the female gendered subject in technoculture in order to point to some tensions that continue to persist both in print and simulation culture.

To conclude, we will return to the polemic concerning new media and the book, a cultural displacement that Deleuze has referred to as the "political assassination" of literature. Is there still space for critical literary practices when the novel is gradually being transformed into the bestseller, an object of consumption to be featured on televised talk shows? If late capitalism is indeed on the verge of murdering literature, the work of Genet, Guibert, and Bouraoui nevertheless offers up an aesthetics of resistance. The conclusion will thus explore the parameters of contemporary modes of resistance in an era where all cultural production traverses, in Wahneema Lubiano's terms, the "slippery ground between reaching people and commodification" (qtd. in Shohat and Stam 340).

NOTES

1. In "Critical Pedagogy and Cyberspace," for example, Lankshear, Peters, and Knobel write: "The status of the book as the text paradigm of modernity underwrites the social construction of school as a quintessential modernist institutional space of enclosure. The book has typically been seen to enclose meaning and experience and, thereby, to promise the possibility of bringing the world into the classroom...the assumption that books and other texts enclose meaning, and that the task of readers is to extract this meaning, legitimates the role of teacher as the presumed authority on matters of interpretation and accuracy" (155). The authors here seek to criticize education as a "space of enclosure," and they suggest that "the book, the classroom and the curriculum can be viewed as intermeshed fixed enclosures which operate in concert to separate educational engagement from wider spheres of social practice" (154).

2. Lankshear, Peters, and Knobel suggest that "the presumptions and deep presuppositions which come with the book as the paradigm form of the text underwrite all modernist educational spaces of enclosure. These, however, are forced into the open and called critically into question in cyberspace—in ways that historically have become inhibited in bookspace. They include the fixity and stability of the word, its left-right/top-down/beginning-end axes of enclosure, the text as an author-controlled environment, the teacher as authoritative bearer of textual meaning (author surrogate), and so on.... The radical interactiveness and convertibility of digital text undermines at the level of lived textual practice the very notion of a static, immutable, transcendent reality pictured by the book" (167).

1 | Simulation Culture and Literature: An Impossible Synthesis?

He who seeks to approach his own buried past must conduct himself like a man digging...He must not be afraid to return again and again to the same matter...For the matter itself is only a deposit, a stratum, which yields only to the most meticulous examination of what constitutes the real treasure hidden within the earth: the images, severed from all earlier associations, that stand—like precious fragments or torsos in a collector's gallery—in the prosaic room of our later understanding.

—Walter Benjamin

If life in the "information age" or postmodernism has already received vast critical attention, it has primarily been from a sociological and philosophical perspective concerned with how the media or the image—from television to the internet to virtual reality—effects contemporary discursive practices as well as contemporary cultures. Unable as yet to achieve a comprehensive understanding of the transformations instigated by the spread of the media, theorists nevertheless agree that a primary modulation has occurred at the level of perception of reality.

With the globalization of the "information superhighway" and the ever-increasing permutation of mass media images into daily life, reality evades representation. The consequences of this phenomenon are far-reaching since it would seem that the media has taken control of the "real." In other words, as media universalizes itself, so does it universalize the space by which it is vehiculated, that is the space of images or the screen. A displacement from representation to simulation is thus operated. Indeed, as many theorists have already maintained, the contemporary period is characterized by simulation to such an extent, reality itself is dissolved leaving in its place a no-place or a hyper-real. Andreas Huyssen's presentation of this particular line of thought in *Twilight Memories* (1995) perhaps best sums up this perspective:

> Postmodern media culture deterritorializes and deconstructs, delocalizes and decodes. It dissolves reality in the simulacrum, makes it vanish behind or rather on the screens of word and image processing machines. What is lost according to this account of a society saturated with images and discourses is not utopia but reality. At stake is the agony of the real, the fading of the senses, the dematerialization of the body, both figuratively and literally. Utopia is no longer needed, or so it is claimed, because all utopias have already fulfilled themselves, and that fulfillment is fatal and catastrophic. (90)

Images today indeed invade reality uncontrollably and with such rapidity, they pose radical challenges to the organization of space and time in contemporary society. According to Georges Balandier, it is by means of a collapsing of space and time that images are able to modulate reality and reconstruct it:

> L'image actuelle bouleverse l'appréhension de la temporalité; elle abolit presque la relation communément établie entre l'espace et le temps, en raison de la rapidité de sa transmission, et la société présente se trouve alors définie comme 'potentiellement sans distance et simultanée'; elle permet l'envahissement par l'événement et, ce faisant, elle contribue à la réduction de toute épaisseur temporelle; elle est l'un des facteurs, par sa nature même, d'une culture consacrant la prévalence de l'éphémère et de l'inachèvement. (19)

One of the most remarkable effects of the collapsing of boundaries and distance in space and time is the confusion of public and private spheres, exterior and interior space. In effect, the borders separating public and private space are more and more permeable due to the increasing connections one can make with the outside from one's own home, office, etc., thanks to telecommunications. A new community thus emerges which, as Balandier would say, is a mere simulacrum, that of "vivre ensemble séparément" (20). This simulated community—created primarily via the screen—explains in large part the contemporary atmosphere of general depoliticization, characterized by a regression of social awareness and a (re)turn to individualism. For as Baudrillard explains in *The Transparency of*

Evil (1993), while the screen simulates direct contact with the other, "the other, the interlocutor, is never really involved: the screen works much like a mirror, for the screen itself as locus of the interface is the prime concern.... This is communication in its purest form, for there is no intimacy here except with the screen, and with an electronic text that is no more than a design filigreed onto life" (12). The screen creates the illusion of transparency since everything is absorbed into the order of the same. The word screen thus retains its etymological meaning as a "curtain" or veil which separates or conceals, for as Baudrillard asserts, in this order of the same, "the Other as gaze, the Other as mirror, the Other as opacity—all are gone" (122).

In this logic, the screen becomes a place of (simulated) violence: in transforming reality into no-place, it also strips space of its cultural specificity and its function to protect. Space in this era of global mediatization, explains Balandier, is modulated by effects of the screen. Submitted to a dialectic of closeness/distance by teledetection systems, space is progressively overtaken by inquiring images which themselves introduce a certain panoptic power (21).

The surveying and recording eye of the media has ostensibly infiltrated modern fiction, most especially contemporary novels. From Jean Echnoz's presentation of characters whose activities are in perfect synchronicity with the movie they are watching on television in *Lac* (1989) to Hervé Guibert's quasi-journalistic portrayals of life mediated through high-tech equipment in *L'Homme au chapeau rouge* (1992), media technologies have definitively operated an evolution in the French novel of the eighties and nineties. Whether it be through references to the banality of everyday life or descriptions of brand-name mass commodity items (e.g., Sony walkmans and Ray Ban sunglasses), the recourse to a non-abstract, "clear" accessible style or the abundance of *non-lieux*,[1] postmodernist writers as various as Anne Garréta, Jean-Philippe Toussaint, Marie Redonnet, Leïla Sebbar and Rachid Boudjedra, among many others, create novels where popular and/or mass culture images are an integral and *necessary* part of narrative—a central discursive paradigm for narrative referential systems.[2] Due to the media's primacy in the social sphere, however, the extent to which the novel still serves as a "mirror of society" risks being overshadowed by its (perceived) capitulation to mass-mediated culture and the attendant alterations to the practice of writing and even of reading.[3]

Indeed, media technologies are often thought to rival, if not supplant, literature and books. Georges Balandier's analysis helps to position the book in the transition from print to simulation culture. Pointing out that "c'est la première fois dans l'histoire des hommes que la réalité proche se trouve immergée par le flux quotidien des images et des messages" (17), Balandier undertakes a discussion of societies before and after modernity (in Benjamin's sense). Significantly, he attributes books to traditional societies or societies not yet inundated with mediology:

> Il se trace une coupure sans cesse élargie entre les sociétés antérieures et celles de la modernité en expansion. Les premières sont, en longue durée, celles de la tradition où l'oralité prévaut en tant que moyen de transmission, puis celles du livre et de la missive. La dernière formation est celle où les réseaux de communication instrumentalisent les rapports sociaux, où la médiatisation est en voie de généralisation et crée un nouvel environnement, si bien que le savoir dont elles sont l'objet devient pour une large part une 'médiologie' (selon le mot de R. Debray). Il ne s'agit pas, à l'évidence, d'un simple changement quantitatif. (8)

In the new environment of mediology, creation itself, whether it be scientific, literary, artistic or purely practical, is dependent on the image. With computers, as Balandier asserts, the image becomes an active partner in the creative endeavor. If it engenders certain advantages—allowing virtually unexplored terrain to be rendered perceptible, for example, as in the practice of medicine—it nevertheless has its limitations since, as Balandier notes, that which is represented by images is in turn defined by the capabilities of the image itself: "L'acte créateur se transforme ainsi; il est nécessairement collectif (vidéographie = graphistes + informaticiens), et il trouve ses limites dans les contraintes du 'système', si bien que l'artiste doit être plus que l'utilisateur de celui-ci, il doit le 'pénétrer' afin d'en exploiter les potentialités" (14).

Surely, books have not simply disappeared in the wake of simulation culture. What precisely is the status of literature and books, then, in this "mediatrix?" One of the pioneers of the avant-garde, the Mexican Nobel laureate Octavio Paz, is certainly not optimistic in response. For in an interview published in 1994 he remarks,

> Literature used to be an extraordinary celebration of those collected feelings, passions, desires and tragedies that endure over time. Just as we used to make cathedrals or palaces to endure for centuries, we also made literature to endure. Every word was chosen very carefully—with very consistent and solid power of meaning—with the intention of duration. But more and more, literature has become cheap, instantaneous entertainment. Now, if they are fortunate enough, modern works of literature have the duration of one season. (1)

Indeed, there is a tendency not only in scholarly writing but also in society to contrast, and inevitably privilege, simulation culture over print culture. In the cultural milieu, as Balandier points to, "les jeunes générations sont celles des 'fils de pub'...ou celles 'du regard' ainsi que le révèle une enquête consacrée à la culture des étudiants—le cinéma, la pub et le rock composent plus que la littérature et l'idéologie leur milieu culturel" (15). In the academic milieu, the argument of Mark Taylor and Esa Saarinen in *Imagologies* (1994) could be considered perhaps the most comprehensive if not symptomatic reflection on the media and contemporary discourses.

Fully embracing the "mediatrix," Taylor and Saarinen set out in *Imagologies* to conduct "a critical and cultural investigation into the functioning and forms of production of the image technologies of our time" ("Virtual Reality" 12).[4] In their line of exploration, thinking in terms of print or textualities is to remain encapsulated in stasis. "In a culture of the simulacrum," they write,

> textuality becomes a cage.... To join the contemporary debate in a way that fulfills the political and ethical promise of critical engagement, it is necessary to adjust to this new condition—even if this means the rejection of the ancient axiom of philosophy according to which the conceptual, the textual and the written are primary. ("Net Effect" 7)

Thoroughly accepting the often heard postulate that "ours is an age of images and simulacra," Taylor and Saarinen hold little hope for the future of literature strictly speaking. Indeed their own project (a self-proclaimed "non-book" written as email) inscribes itself in the moment of transition from print to electronic culture; one of its primary points is to relay the message, "[i]f you read books, justify it" ("Superficiality" 11). Moreover, in their view, "critique that is restricted to the realm of the literate and remains a literary project is no longer feasible as an effective strategy for action.... Literate reason and the literary critic have become relics of the past" ("Media Philosophy" 17).

Taylor and Saarinen base their critique of print culture within a larger critique of the academy, which is, in their eyes, "confinement within the culture of expertise" ("Ending the Academy" 5). Out of touch with the masses,

> Institutions of higher education have not taken advantage of the resources and energies circulating beyond the walls of the academy.... Enlightenment no longer automatically sells. Nor does critical thought. To sell your product, you must get down to business and take advertising and marketing seriously. The discourses of scholarly achievement not only define the wrong agenda but have no promotional strategy. If reason is to be practical in simcult, it must be electrified. ("Ending" 9)

In this logic, the name of the game is speed, a recurrent (positive) notion in *Imagologies*.

While Taylor and Saarinen see the end of the academy (and alongside it the erasure of the distinction between elite and mass culture) as cultural pragmatism, one of whose primary tools is speed, speed, according to Gilles Deleuze, is precisely that which nourishes the crisis in contemporary literature:

> The system of bestsellers is a system of rapid turnover. Many bookshops are already becoming like the record shops that only stock things that make it into the charts. This is what *Apostrophes* is all about. Fast turnover necessarily means selling people what they expect: even what's 'daring,' 'scandalous,' strange, and so on falls into the market's predictable forms. The conditions for literary creation, which emerge only unpredictably, with a slow turnover and progressive recognition, are fragile.... (*Negotiations* 128)

In the system of bestsellers, literature truly becomes a co-partner with the image. *Apostrophes* is precisely about creating literature as a marketable object-image of consumption via television. Let us recall that for Balandier, the image in such partnerships tends to take the upper hand, limiting representation by its own defining characteristics.[5] In the case of literature-as-mass commodity, speed would thus become the restricting mechanism that necessarily forgoes the literary enterprise, for as Deleuze remarks, "books become 'secondary' when marketing takes over" (130), amounting more or less to "literature as light entertainment" (128). Indeed, as Deleuze's comments make clear, literature can and should find its place alongside simulation culture,

> For if audiovisual media ever replace literature, it won't be as competing means of expression, but as a monopoly of structures that also stifle the creative possibilities in those media themselves. If literature dies, it will be a violent death, a political assassination (as in the USSR, even if nobody notices). It's not a matter of comparing different sorts of medium. The choice isn't between written literature and audiovisual media. It's between creative forces (in audiovisual media as well as literature) and domesticating forces. It's highly unlikely that audiovisual media will find the conditions for creation once they've been lost in literature. Different modes of expression may have different creative possibilities, but they're all related insofar as they must counter the introduction of a cultural space of markets and conformity—that is, a space of 'producing for the market'—together. (*Negotiations* 131)

From this perspective, it is evident that literature and simcult can and do coexist although the extent to which either resists cultural spaces of conformity today is up for investigation. In effect, outside the domain of science fiction, much remains to be done concerning the interactions between contemporary literary creation and current media technologies. Faced with the onslaught of on-line, easily accessible information/entertainment which requires little memory and little imagination, literature's place in the contemporary era is at best unstable. This instability has, in turn, lead to a certain impasse within literary theory and criticism. It is not surprising, then, that inquiries into the current status of the literary text often succumb "to a fascination with apocalyptic discussions[,] react[ing] with panic at prognostications that the book is about to disappear" (Eco 17).

The debate we have been discussing thus far over the predicted "death" of literature at the hands of electronic media at the end of the twentieth century testifies to the critic's need to reposition the literary text in relation to mass culture. Indeed, one of the main concerns for literary critics today is the place literary works occupy in a world overwhelmed by technological advances.[6] This concern is less a matter of the age-old cliché concerning the "end" of art than it is the work of art's status in the contemporary world where, in line with the "culture of the simulacrum" described above, literary works can find no place and therefore no meaning. In Alain Finkielkraut's terms, which echo those of Octavio Paz and Gilles Deleuze,

> Le problème auquel nous sommes, depuis peu, confrontés est différent, et plus grave: les oeuvres existent, mais la frontière entre la culture et le divertissement s'étant estompée, il n'y a plus de lieu pour les accueillir et pour leur donner sens. Elles flottent donc absurdement dans un espace sans coordonnées ni repères. Quand la haine de la culture devient elle-même culturelle, la vie avec la pensée perd toute signification. (158)

In order to better understand the parameters of the space of literature today, it is necessary to position literature within a broad perspective that takes into account the importance of technologies in the contemporary world on the one hand, and a specific analysis of the use of these technologies by twentieth-century writers on the other, i.e. what effect is sought and to what end are they being exploited?

To this end, a more affirmative avenue of inquiry into fiction writing today does exist, which consists of an exploration of literature's status as (historiographic or postmodernist) metafiction.[7] Some of its central defining characteristics are the use of cinematic and photographic models, as well as a crisscrossing of the borders between high art and mass or popular culture and those between the discourses of art and the discourses of the world. Although analyses of historiographic metafiction bring the importance of mass culture to the fore, within this current of literary criticism the role of the screen is still left undertreated, subordinated as it were to larger problematics such as the politics of narrative representation and the high art/mass culture dichotomy.

For my part, I agree with Andreas Huyssen's estimation that the impact of various technologies has been the determining factor in the evolution of the work of art in both modernism and postmodernism, producing what he refers to as the "technological imagination."[8] In order to grasp the position of the space of literature within our contemporary image culture today, then, we must first take a closer theoretical look at how the screen has transformed daily life. Only then will we be in a position to evaluate literature's status in relation to current technologies and to highlight ways in which literature approximates some of the same experiences evoked by technologies such as cinema and virtual reality.

Masses and Media

In line with the mediatization of everyday life today, daily contact with the screen is virtually unavoidable for most people.[9] In the literal sense, we watch the screen of our televisions or computers as well as the "silver screen" of the cinema. Moreover, we increasingly encounter the screen at music concerts, art exhibits, and even in the classroom. In a more figurative sense, we meet the screen in the form of printed press, telephone answering machines (with which, precisely, we may "screen" our calls), radios, adverts, and faxing devices. Indeed, like the film actress in Hervé Guibert's short story *Copyright, cinéma* (1994) who is being stalked by a murderer "for real" yet who continually blurs the lines between fact and fiction, it is becoming increasingly difficult to separate the activities of our own daily lives from those that occur on screen: "Elle a peur, et pourtant elle a déjà été poursuivie plusieurs fois dans des films, plusieurs fois elle a été la victime d'un maniaque, et elle s'en est toujours sortie" (*La Piqûre d'amour* 21).

This blurring of reality and fiction referred to so often today is in fact inherent to the media themselves, as Pierre Sorlin describes:

> The media put daily concerns and fictional, but not unbelievable, situations side by side and then, by interrupting the former with adverts and the latter with news, blur the seemingly well-established distinction between the 'genres.' It is no wonder that the one adopts the vocabulary

of the other and that fictional characters are taken as being illustrations of
social change or backwardness. (66)

The superposition of media fictions with everyday reality is in itself *not*
the problem with the media, however; nor is it to be confused with the
media's power to manipulate the masses. After all, the ways in which
audiences work with the messages and images generated by the media are
highly dynamic and indeterminate. In fact, whereas the hyperrealist
approach to the media postulates that, in Baudrillard's terms, "one's
response to the image on the screen is not the aesthetic response of an
observation characterized by distance, judgment and pleasure" (Zurbrugg
288), recent sociological and/or ethnographic media studies assert just the
opposite. Indeed, when people's use of the media is situated in domestic
space and organized within the dynamics of domestic relations, the
audience's connection to the media is no longer perceived as a passive one.
Thus Roger Silverstone writes that "the effort to persuade and to please
which television mobilizes in the metaphors of its rhetoric creates a space
for response, but there is no telling in any individual situation what that
response will be" (90). Pierre Sorlin similarly maintains that "To a large
extent, the use of the media is inspired by the matrix of pleasure and desire.
Audiences cannot be seen as millions of ears and eyes absorbing attentively
what they are offered. Not only do they evaluate and criticize, but they
intervene more actively by taking pleasure..." (82).

This is not to suggest that the part mass media play in perpetuating
the system of power is to be ignored or discounted.[10] Nor am I suggesting
that the hyperrealist (Baudrillardian) account of the media described above
is inappropriate or misleading, since it does chronicle many modulations in
the contemporary episteme relative to memory, simultaneity and
temporality.[11] What is clear, however, is that this approach to a large extent
forecloses the audience's space for negotiation with the media, a space that
necessarily persists despite (in spite of?) the media's homogenizing and
hyperreal effects.[12]

Due to the omnipotence of simulation culture—characterized by "the
psychic bombardment of the spectacular in nearly every aspect" of our life
(Pfeil 57)—it is easy to see why spectatorship has been divorced for many

from a critical engagement with the real world. After all, "since in the world of simulacra discourses become more and more 'real'" (Talens 21), everything has seemingly passed into fiction (that produced by the market) thereby displacing and even obliterating the very notion of fiction itself. As Nicole Brossard, a contemporary writer from Québec has asked,

> What is fiction now that 'reality shows'—those dramatizations of real stories about serial killers—provide all the details we wanted to know about sex, violence, and injustice? What is fiction when, through technology, a grandmother can bear and give birth to her daughter's child? (Huffer, "An Interview with Nicole Brossard," 116)

As Brossard's comments testify, writers are forced to contend with the media's position as the symbolic core of many—if not most—social worlds.[13] It therefore seems appropriate to recognize and re-evaluate (rather than simply derogate) the extent to which the formal aspects of the media as well as their social uses have had a part in shaping writers' approaches to fiction writing, whether it be fiction written for the market (i.e., the bestseller system) or other more resistent modes of fiction. Indeed, perhaps now more than ever, as Andreas Huyssen explains,

> we have to begin to make other kinds of distinctions among a growing body of works and artistic practices that position themselves quite critically and pointedly in contemporary culture, in terms of their relation to the market and the institutions, their specific aesthetic strategies, and their claims on different groups of readers and spectators. (*Twilight Memories* 96)

But what of the specificity of fictions generated by—if not originating in—the media themselves? Marc Guillaume, a sociologist who focuses on the social meaning of the active use of telecommunications, helps us to explore this question through his analysis of the subject of new forms of telecommunications, a mode he calls "spectrality." Guillaume's analysis is significant to my readings of Genet, Guibert, and Bouraoui in the following chapters because he postulates a model of spectatorship that is highly relevant to the articulation of both subjectivity and death in these author's texts. His analysis, moreover, helps us to align literature with the very mediums that have supposedly displaced it (e.g., cyberspace and virtual reality), thus furthering our premise that literary space serves a critical and theoretical function within image culture. I turn now, then, to Guillaume's examination of spectatorship in the electronic age.

Ghost in the Machine or The "Carnival of Spectres"

New forms of media technology—what Guillaume calls "la télématique" (telephone + "informatique")—produce in turn new forms of sociality in technoculture. As face-to-face interactions are increasingly substituted by telecommunications, a whole symbolic array of traditional forms of sociability undergoes immense change (Raz and Shapira 424).[14] These changes involve not only people's interactions with each other and with machines, but also mutations within technology itself. In contradistinction to early communication models, teletechnologies today invite people more and more to involve themselves directly (albeit anonymously) in the scenarios being presented. As Guillaume explains, where once communication operated according to two distinct models— irradiation (one-way communication such as that of the mass media) and contagion (interactive sequential communication such as telephones, rumors, and movements of opinion)—modern teletechnologies now hybridize them, thus creating communication models which are also commutative ones:

> La puissance informatique des centres serveurs et la souplesse d'utilisation du réseau téléphonique permettent en effet de réaliser à la fois des liaisons interactives et irradiantes: chacun peut choisir son correspondant et en changer à volonté, la communication se double d'une commutation. (78)

Going beyond the mere blurring of fact and fiction typical of traditional media, this hybridization has the capacity to create fictions endowed with a new force since within these forms, spectators can become actors in the double sense of the word: not only do they have the ability to enter into the space of the medium and partcipate in the communications it facilitates, but they also gain access to a space in which role play and the wearing of masks reign supreme. Significantly, in this realm of computer-mediated communication, users appear to each other primarily through explicit written language. They thus possess the "literary" capability to project their personalities in written texts. For Guillaume, it is precisely this projection that de-composes the subject and turns him or her into a spectral image:

> Dans de tels rapport conviviaux...chacun fait l'expérience d'une sorte d'évanouissement (*fading*) de son moi propre.... Derrière les mots et les images il existe certes des sujets, mais ceux-ci n'ont délégue sur les écrans qu'une fraction (fiction) d'eux-mêmes, désincarnée et déresponsabilisée: ils se projettent comme spectres. (81)

In our discussion of Genet, Guibert and Bouraoui, we will see that image technologies facilitate a similar dispersal of subjectivity in these authors' texts. The space of literature thus approximates the space of virtual reality insofar as both mediums permit subjects to shed the symbolic constraints of identity necessary in everyday life in order to project themselves into a new image.[15] Far from alienating the subject, the type of anonymity afforded by both the literary text and the media opens onto a certain freedom (a way to release the subject from oppressive institutionally defined subjectivites) and thus to a joyful communion in the carnival of spectres:[16]

> Le réseau télématique [et littéraire], à l'image de la très grande ville, permet des communications à intensité variable et à identité flottante. Il garantit en particulier l'anonymat et favorise donc une certaine forme d'anomie— car le *nomen* est la première condition du *nomos*. Mais cette anomie n'est pas génératrice d'exclusion et de déstructuration sociales. A l'opposé des critiques naïves de l'anomie, issues des hypothèses de Durkheim, elle serait plutôt vecue sur un mode jubilatoire, comme ouverture sur un espace de liberté et de nomadisme permettant tous les jeux de masque et de rôle possibles. (Guillaume 81)

In Guillaume's view, teletechnologies provide not only ways to counteract the homogenizing effects of other media, but also a new means by which individuals can control their self-presentation. It is precisely at this level—the level where subjects may negotiate identity while creating alliances that can transcend the confines of class, race, gender, regional and national culture—that the current media harbor a radical *potential* which allows for not only new constructions of notions of subjectivity and fiction, but also of the political. Lankshear, Peters, and Knobel, for example, link cyberspace environments to the discovery of "the contingency of human identity and the ever present possibilities for actively taking up and constructing new identities" (176). As they further explain, within these environments

> learners can be freed to approach their identities and lives as being subject in interesting ways to their 'own authorship:' within the bounds of these identity-constitutive social practices/Discourses they choose to engage.... The relationship between identities and discursive practices can be uncovered and made explicit relatively easily in cyberspace. Exploring subjectivity and experimenting with possibilities for identity are always a matter of relating the personal to the discursive. In these ways cyberspace can be seen to offer enhanced access to important forms of meta-level understandings of social practices in relation to subjectivity, identity, and agency (or agenthood). (176)

This is not to suggest that cyberspace environments by their very nature automatically engender transformative social practices; indeed, as with media spectatorship in postmodern culture in general, these spaces are politically ambivalent. Transformative or resistant readings, therefore,

> depend on a certain cultural or political preparation that 'primes' the spectator [user] to read critically.... [W]hile disempowered communities can decode dominant programming through a resistant perspective, they can only do so to the extent that their collective life and historical memory have provided an alternative framework of understanding. (Shohat and Stam 354)

The texts of Genet, Guibert, and Bouraoui, alongside other models of postmodernist fiction, provide this type of priming in their presentations of dominant media perspectives from multiple alternative viewpoints. Enacting the spectral identity described above by Guillaume, they present subjects who, in the face of dominant cultural constructions of identity, interpret culture against the grain through the lens of personal experience. Their texts can be understood, in this sense, as a place of resistance.

With the breakdown of collective identities articulated around the imaginary community of nation or the international brotherhood of socialist *man*, people are searching for new modes of aesthetic and political experience more in tune with their personal experience. The transfigured "public realm" established by transnational communications networks, as it offers both new forms of alliance and contestation (Hebdige 233), appears to be the preferred mode by which to conceptualize new ideas of community. Indeed, as Dick Hebdige remarks, transnational media systems do have tremendous binding power and today, perhaps more than any other medium, they are able to capture audiences' yearning for community whether it be for the better (as in the Free Mandela movement) or for the worse (as in televangelism) (233). Pierre Sorlin maintains to the same effect that co-operation is the most significant outcome of the use of the media, for "[s]haring the same means of information, circulating them, discussing them creates an attachment to the group as a whole. In this respect, the content of media is important but less in itself than through the unifying effect it provokes" (36).

The powers of mobilization specific to the information age—that is the media's ability to tap into audiences' desire to "feel *connected* to a transitory mass of other people, to engage in transitory and *superficial* alliances" (Hebdige 233)—suggests the need for a new approach not only to how we conceptualize and discuss culture and history, but literary texts as well. In our analysis of spectrality, a theoretical model that helps to explain the contradictory modes of contemporary subjectivities and identities, we have seen that both literary texts and cyberspace environments offer the powers of transitory *alteration* (i.e., the alterity of "je est un autre," a paradigm drawn, significantly, from the *poetics* of Rimbaud). As Guillaume further explains,

> Derrière les spectres [readers/spectators] anonymes et anomiques, subsistent des sujets ordinaires qui ont une demande traditionnelle d'identité, de racines, d'abri symbolique et des attitudes d'individualisme exacerbé. Mais l'expérience de la spectralité leur apprend que l'espace social se double d'un espace imaginaire dont la métrique est singulière: le plus lointain, l'inconnu, l'étranger peut devenir le plus proche, celui auquel on se confie le plus intimement…. Elle leur apprend aussi que dans tout rapport à l'autre, et pas seulement dans la communication médiatisée, le moi est une construction fictive (je est un autre). Et surtout que le réel du

corps et de sa finitude n'est supportable qu'à travers le recours à l'imaginaire. (81)

The prevailing argument concerning literature today undervalues its relationship to new media and assumes too readily that because literary space is closely patterned after commercial/marketing considerations, it has been displaced by them. Contemporary approaches to fiction must remain informed, however, by a methodology which considers the intricacies of the discursive spaces which construct literature as an object (of study *or* of consumption).[17] Throughout the remainder of this chapter, and in my readings of Genet, Guibert, and Bouraoui, I do not attempt to provide a definitive solution to this problem. Rather, I hope to bring into focus some critical directions that could help trace out new approaches to literary space in the electronic age. I turn now, then, to a closer look at the specificity of fiction writing today and to how Genet, Guibert, and Bouraoui respond to the challenges of image culture.

Contemporary Fiction(s) and Writers: Literature as "Variable Reality"

Contemporary works of fiction—referred to in criticism alternately as metafictions, hybrid fictions or postmodernist fictions due to their blurring of the lines between the real and the fake—inscribe themselves in an already well-developed trend among audiences to prefer works that are anchored in personal, everyday life experience. Like media, these fictions act as a kind of

> intermediate sector between the concrete area where people act daily and the problems, or concerns, or worries which are present, important to them although they can only reach them obliquely; [they] represent the transition from one sphere to the other; they provide a real experience, the experience of viewing or reading, which is also of an indirect, imaginary nature. (Sorlin 60)

Indeed, as Guillaume points to, works of pure fiction—whether they be literary, cinematographic or televisual—are rivaled to a greater and greater extent by hybrid fictions or fictions that make use of what Jean

Ricardou has called "variable reality," that is "the strategy whereby a supposedly 'real' representation is revealed to have been merely 'virtual'— an illusion or secondary representation, a representation within the representation—or vice versa, a supposedly virtual representation is shown to have been 'really real' after all" (qtd. in McHale 116). Indeed, if in this *fin de siècle* people in mass numbers are seeking out stories that are anchored in "real life" or that convey personal confessions relative to their curiosity (and/or fears) about other people (and even about themselves), this quest for the "live" event, precipitated by the overwhelming presence of the media in our lives, nevertheless remains illusory. For as Pierre Sorlin describes, "In itself our world is already a whole, an omnipresent plenitude. And yet the media attempt at replacing it. Not only do they reduplicate it but, in many respects, they substitute it: *a good many people watch television to see what they could witness in the street*" (60, my emphasis).

It is undeniable that this trend, fueled by the media, is responsible on the one hand for the regression to narrative, subjectivity, identity, and authenticity in recent literary production. Some examples include the penchant for autobiography (many of them written by leading intellectuals) and confessional texts. Yet on the other hand, as we will see, certain writers like Genet, Guibert and Bouraoui inscribe this trend only to subvert it. In other words, they draw on the mobilizing power of personal confession to draw readers in, and then proceed to shift the narrative focalization by dispersing the author-subject into different figures thus encouraging forms of "surrogate subjectivity" (McHale 202) akin to those described in cyberspace environments. Through elaborate mechanisms of distanciation and identification typical to media technologies, then, these authors' texts replicate the processes modern readers have become accustomed to through their own uses of media, but deploy those same processes toward new understandings of subjectivity, not to mention gender, sexuality, and history. In short, these fictions utilize the sheen and confessional modes of the media in order to engender the experience of spectrality described above.

As I described in the prologue, Genet's, Guibert's and Bouraoui's fictions, like those specific to teletechnologies, inscribe themselves directly in the writing subject's encounter with the screen. The reader, moved into and out of various subject positions through identification with the narrator, becomes implicated in the process. These fictions are thus interactive in a wide sense since they directly address readers as spectators *and actors* within the textual space. We also recall here that as the (writing) subject enacts spectral identity, a space of performative liberation is opened where alterity, rather than vanishing, circulates freely in a carnivalesque atmosphere, and even manifests itself in its most radical form: death.

To Simulate is to Learn to Die: Literature as a (Postmodernist) Space of Resurrection

It comes as no surprise that death should figure as a central element in fiction written in the era of mediatization. After all, as John Berger remarks, "[l]es images explosives pleines de violence sont partout" ("Un système" 97). From one perspective, audiences are lead by the sheer number of violent images to a certain indifference toward pain since with the production of death-as-spectacle, the body becomes a mere simulacrum thereby obliterating suffering. As Berger explains, while the image of death is everywhere, "très rares sont les images de souffrance. Comment pourrait-il y avoir souffrance s'il n'y a pas de corps? Ici réside la dure perversité du spectacle offert par le système. La violence, oui. Mais pas la souffrance" ("Un système" 97). Death is reduced here to a mere "effet de réel" and thus has no more import than a video-game or a photograph. Hence Baudrillard writes that "The consummate enjoyment of the signs of guilt, despair, violence, and death are replacing guilt, anxiety, and even death in the total euphoria of simulation. This euphoria aims to abolish cause and effect, origin and end, and replace them with reduplication" (*Symbolic Exchange and Death* 72).

The disappearance of the reality of death and its replacement by the consumer (entertainment/military) image is specific to the processes of Western modernity. Already in 1936, Walter Benjamin had linked the decline of both storytelling and the presence of death in everyday life to new forms of technology and communication in modernity. Pointing out that "If the art of storytelling has become rare, the dissemination of information has had a decisive share in this state of affairs," Benjamin proceeds to the conclusion that information technologies have altered not only the communication of experience, but the idea of eternity—and therefore death—as well: "The idea of eternity has ever had its strongest source in death. If this idea declines, so we reason, the face of death must have changed. It turns out that this change is identical with the one that has diminished the communicability of experience to the same extent as the art of storytelling had declined" (93). This phenomenon, we recall, can be linked to the telescoping effect media technologies have on space and time or, in other words, memories.

The decline of memory and a sense of the past (i.e., the alteration of experience) coupled with advanced medical technology in bourgeois society instigated the expulsion of death from everyday life into the imaginary, depriving it of its real effects. Subsequently, death was "cleansed" of its more abject qualities and erased from view.

> Dying was once a public process in the life of the individual and a most exemplary one; think of the medieval pictures in which the deathbed has turned into a throne toward which the people press through the wide-open doors of the death house. In the course of modern times dying has been pushed further and further out of the perceptual world of the living. There used to be no house, hardly a room, in which someone had not once died…. Today people live in rooms that have never been touched by death, dry dwellers of eternity, and when their end approaches they are stowed away in sanatoria or hospitals by their heirs. (Benjamin 93)

This eradication of death from the social/symbolic sphere in Western culture has had a decisive impact. Baudrillard has shown, for example, that the expulsion of the dead from the group of the living which accompanied the trajectory of reason in modernity in fact models all other forms of social exclusion: "At the very core of the 'rationality' of our culture," he writes, "is an exclusion that precedes every other, more radical than the exclusion of madmen, children or inferior races, an exclusion preceding all these and serving as their model, the exclusion of the dead and of death" (*Symbolic Exchange* 126). The eradication of death and the dead in this sense amounts to the eradication of alterity, a first act of power that inevitably seeks further social control:

> Power is established on death's borders. It will subsequently be sustained by further separations (the soul and the body, the male and the female, good and evil, etc.) that have infinite ramifications, but the principal separation is between life and death.... This is precisely the way in which power will later be instituted between the subject separated from its body, between the individual separated from its social body, between man separated from his labour: the agency of mediation and representation flourishes in this rupture. (*Symbolic Exchange* 130)

The separation of life and death, then, relegates death to the domain of the un-real (it becomes Other), and sets up a hierarchical system of representation based on the exclusion of alterity. By keeping death outside the circuits of symbolic exchange, power is thus able to neutralize the former's radicality and maintain its own hold over the social sphere.

Culture's attitude toward death has manifested itself throughout the ages in literature. We have seen that from one perspective, death in the information age has been replaced by its sign/image, leading to death's further marginalization in technoculture through the obliteration of the body and suffering. Paradoxically, however, in postmodernist literature and representation death is the object of renewed interest, finding itself at the center of fiction writing.[18] Similarly, in the narratives of Genet, Guibert, and Bouraoui, as we will see, personal experiences of and with death produce a space of critical reflection which, in turn, allows for alternative readings of dominant cultural representations. Could it be that the very power that expels death from the social realm—that is, the culture industry—simultaneously creates a space for death's expression in literature? I would answer yes. And the way this is accomplished is through the contradictory powers of the image.

Images, as we discussed above, have always been recognized as a source of both fascination and deception, powerful agents capable of evil deeds. Ever since Plato, warnings against their seductive ruses have poured forth. As Steven Shaviro summarizes this line of argument,

Images are false, since they have been separated from the real situations of which they claim to be the representations, as well as from the material conditions in which they have been produced. They are suspect, unreliable, and 'ideological,' because they presume to subsist in this state of alienation, and even perpetuate it by giving rise to delusive 'reality effects,' rituals of disavowal, and compensatory fantasies of plenitude and possession. (17)

Today, the image's power of seduction has supposedly won over, leaving us stranded as it were in a land of insubstantial projections (the hyperreal) bereft of meaning. But what if it were precisely the image's very insubstantiality—its quality of being neither here nor there, neither true nor false, neither real nor artificial—at the source of its radical power, a power that is closely linked not only to subjectivity but also to death? Such is the premise I shall attempt to illustrate in my readings of Genet, Guibert, and Bouraoui. Before doing so, however, we must first turn to the work of Maurice Blanchot which suggests a radical conjuncture between the powers of the image and death, a mode he refers to as fascination. In fact, for Blanchot, it is the particular constellation of fascination, writing, and death that makes the space of literature (and/or art) possible.[19]

Fascination: Spectral Subjects and the Transgression of Identity

"The writer," says Blanchot, "is one who writes in order to be able to die, and he is one whose power to write comes from an anticipated relation with death" (*The Space of Literature* 93). In addressing the paradoxical situation of "'creators' engaged in a profound relation with death" (95), Blanchot is lead to pose the question, Can I die? It is at this level, the level of the (im)possibility of death, that the image (a simulacrum or site of fascination) enters into Blanchot's thoughts on the relationship between the writing subject, death, and literary space. In the following passage, death as Blanchot defines it closely approximates the qualities of the image. In other words, here both death and images are "flat and insubstantial, devoid of interiority and substance, unable to express anything beyond themselves.

They are—frustratingly—static and evanescent at once, too massively present in their very impalpability" (Shaviro 16). Blanchot writes,

> At first glance, the preoccupation of the writer who writes in order to be able to die is an affront to common sense. It would seem we can be sure of at least one event: it will come without any approach on our part, without our bestirring ourselves at all; yes it will come. That is true, but at the same time it is not true, and indeed quite possibly it lacks truth altogether. *At least it does not have the kind of truth which we feel in the world, which is the measure of our action and of our presence in the world.* What makes me disappear from the world cannot find its guarantee there; and thus, in a way, having no guarantee, it is not certain. This explains why no one is linked to death [or the image] by *real* certitude. No one is sure of dying. No one doubts death, but no one can think of certain death except doubtfully. For to think of death is to introduce into thought the supremely doubtful, the brittleness of the unsure…This in itself indicates that if men in general do not think about death, if they avoid confronting it, it is doubtless in order to flee death and hide from it, but that *this escape is possible only because death itself is perpetual flight before death, and because it is the deep of dissimulation.* (*Space* 95, my emphasis)

By claiming that indeed death is not *real* (that is "it does not have the kind of truth which we feel in the world, which is the measure of our action and of our presence in the world") and that death always involves a circular movement of deception ("death is a perpetual flight before death"), Blanchot likens death to a simulated image. In the face of death—just as in the face of the image in Baudrillard's sense—we can only ever be passive since we can never experience death *in its reality* and thus we can never gain mastery over it. It is for this reason that Blanchot continually returns to the same question, one which is explicitly linked to the power of the (writing) subject in the face of death: "Do I myself die, or do I not rather die always other from myself, so that I would have to say that properly speaking *I* do not die? Can I die? Have I the power to die?" (*Space* 98).

Death as a simulated image becomes even more clear in Blanchot's "Two Versions of the Imaginary," where he assimilates the strange power of the image to that of a cadaver. It is interesting to note that in the following description, the primary function of the image/cadaver is to create a point of reference that is a simulacrum:

The image does not, at first glance, resemble the corpse, but the cadaver's strangeness is perhaps also that of the image. What we call mortal remains escapes common categories. *Something is there before us which is not really the living person, nor is it any reality at all. It is neither the same as the person who was alive, nor is it another person, nor is it anything else.* What is there, with the absolute calm of something that has found its place, does not, however, succeed in being convincingly here. Death suspends the relation to place, even though the deceased rests heavily in his spot as if upon the only basis that is left him. To be precise, this basis lacks, the place is missing, the corpse is not in its place. Where is it? It is not here, and yet it is not anywhere else. Nowhere? But then nowhere is here. *The cadaverous presence establishes a relation between here and nowhere.* (*Space* 256, my emphasis)

For both Baudrillard and Blanchot, then, the image is indeed that "cadaverous presence" which paradoxically puts us into a space of passive fascination: between here and nowhere, between reality and fiction, between the real and the fake. But whereas Baudrillard links this passive fascination to the victory of the culture industry over the image and symbolic exchange with death, Blanchot sees the image—a "formless weight of being present in absence"—as that which allows death to subsist in residual form through the fascinating effects of simulation (Gregg 29).[20]

For Blanchot, then, the fascination experienced in front of the image is linked not to the ectasy of total communication subjects experience in the domain of the hyperreal (a position of illusory mastery). Rather, it is linked to an ectasy of a different kind, that is the *momentary* and fleeting dissolution of the subject brought about by its (masochistic) submission to the image/death, which, through its power to seize the subject and overtake it, initiates the transformation from the personal to the impersonal:

> Vivre un événement en image, ce n'est pas avoir de cet événement une image, ni non plus lui donner la gratuité de l'imaginaire…. Ce qui arrive nous saisit comme nous saisirait l'image, c'est-à-dire nous dessasisit, de lui et de nous, nous tient au dehors, fait de ce dehors une présence ou 'Je' ne 'se' reconnaît pas. (*Space* 357, my emphasis)

Similar to the image's function in Guillaume's model of spectrality, the image for Blanchot separates the subject from his or her own fixed identity via its power to fascinate the subject and alter his or her relation not only to

the real, but also to himself or herself. Fascination in the image sphere, in
its rupturing of the notion of a unified, originary and stable subjectivity,
thus becomes a critical tool (contrary to its more widely accepted
connotations) for as John Gregg explains,[21]

> Fascination is not of the order of discursive knowledge.... *It implies a
> temporary interruption of the habitual modes in which subjects perceive themselves and
> the world....* Fascination plays havoc with our conventional sense of time.
> Just as it contests the ontological principle of self-identity and the
> aesthetic notions of original and copy, fascination disrupts linear models
> of temporality which posit a beginning, a process of becoming, and an
> end. There is neither an *arche* nor a *telos* in the universe of fascination and
> resemblance, and repetition comes to take the place of dialectical process.
> (28, my emphasis)

The image sphere, no matter how "inflated," "commodified," and
"betrayed," remains in this sense a site of struggle (Abbas 49). As Blanchot
and Guillaume demonstrate, subjects willing to succumb to a state of
fascination may access this space of "liminality" closely akin to death
through their encounters with the image (whether it be digital *or* written), a
space where "ambivalences, resistances, slippages, dissimulations, doubling,
and even subversions of the cultural codes" become possible (qtd. in
Shohat and Stam 354).

Such is the space opened through the screen in the fiction of Genet,
Guibert, and Bouraoui. In effect, for these authors as for Blanchot,
fascination with the image counteracts the constraining effects of power
since it "breaks down the usual distinction between interiority and
exteriority" (Gregg 28), the living and the dead, self and other, and leads to
a point where the writing subject "becomes estranged from the identity he
[or she] possesses...in the everyday" (Gregg 166). This estrangement, or
what Blanchot calls an "initial doubling," allows the subject to negotiate
with identity *through the transgression of its limits,* a process that is initiated
when the subject, caught up in a state of fascination, splits into another
subject, or what I call a spectral subject:

> The transition from the personal to the impersonal inherent in the writer's
> approach to the space of literature dictates that he become estranged from
> the identity he possesses in the regional economy of the everyday, a *moi*

that, for Blanchot, is 'par avance fracturé,' and *that he become involved with an elusive impersonal spontaneity.* The approach to/of alterity in proximity thus opens up a wound in the self that has been there since time immemorial...which the regional economy must overlook. This 'initial doubling,' a rift within closure that signals a rapport of non-coincidence with itself, renders possible the notion of an integral subject while at the same time undermining its pretensions to primacy. (Gregg 166, my emphasis)

Blanchot's conception of the "initial doubling" subjects undergo when they accept to be drawn into the space where alterity (the image/death) approaches bears affinities with Michel Foucault's conception of "arts of existence" or "techniques of the self."[22] In effect, both theorists posit the transgression of a unified, stable subjectivity as a necessary step toward critical, alternative, and open modes of thought, that is modes of thought constructed without reference to "universal truths and reason" (Simons 122). This concern for the self should not be relegated to the domain of aesthetics strictly speaking, but rather should be viewed as an *aesthetics of political existence* meant to challenge modern political rationality. As Jon Simons explains,

Foucault's genealogies of the subject indicate that individuals are constituted from the start in ways that correlate with social norms. The fabric of society is woven out of relations that both require certain types of individuals and more or less succeed in producing them. If Foucault is right, then attempts to resist current modes of subjection entail opposing networks of power and rationalites of government. Efforts to promote new subjectivities require that alternative modes of government be instituted by refashioning contemporary ones. Hence the promotion of new subjectivities is not merely an ethical question, but also 'political, ...social, philosophical.' (103)

Literary space, like cyberspace today, is indeed a privileged space for the conception and creation of polyvocal, spectral subjects that transgress the conventional boundaries of self-identity.[23] The fiction of Genet, Guibert, and Bouraoui, as we shall explore in the following chapters, harnasses the powers of the screen/image to push the subject into the farthest reaches of the real, and therefore into the unknown. It thus constitutes itself as a political and aesthetic practice of transgression.

NOTES

1. *Non-lieux* are defined by Marc Augé as places of transit—neutral, banal and uniform spaces without history such as airports, train stations, supermarkets, hotels, standardized buildings etc. For a more in-depth discussion of *non-lieux* and their position in "surmodernité," see Augé's *Non-lieux. Introduction à une anthropologie de la surmodernité.*

2. I refer the reader here to several studies on the contemporary novel in France and elsewhere that address some of its central features. Those especially relevant to my topic include Dominique Fisher's "Les non-lieux de Jean-Philippe Toussaint: bricol(l)age textuel et rhétorique du neutre;" Martine Antle's introduction to a collection of essays entitled *The Object in France Today;* Ginette Michaud's "Récits postmodernes?"; Yvan Leclerc's "Autour de Minuit;" Dina Sherzer's "Effets d'intertextualité dans *Shérazade* et *Les Carnets de Shérazade* de Leïla Sebbar;" Brian McHale's *Postmodernist Fiction,* and Linda Hutcheon's *The Politics of Postmodernism.*

3. For a more in-depth analysis of this aspect of postmodernism, see Ben Agger's "*The Decline of Discourse: Reading, Writing and Resistance in Postmodern Capitalism,*" as well as William Nericcio's article "Artif[r]acture: Virulent Pictures, Graphic Narrative and the Ideology of the Visual."

4. I draw the reader's attention here to the unconventional form, both bibliographically and scholarly, of *Imagologies.* This "book" is indeed divided into sections which could be called chapters. However, instead of continual pagination which would facilitate bibliographic citations, each section is numbered independently beginning from the number 1. The reader will note, therefore, that whenever I have cited from this "book," the corresponding section and page number will follow.

5. Ben Agger takes this point even further by drawing out the implications in terms of power and capital: "Power protects, and thus reproduces, itself through media; differential access to communication outlets both parallels and reinforces differential access to wealth and political power. By now, in a televisionized polity, these facts are unsurprising. Yet much political sophistry bemoaning the collapse of 'traditional' public and personal values seems to disregard them: it is ludicrous to argue for 'great books' when people cannot and do not read any books—when textuality, for them, is techno-political imagery screened in the Americanized global village" (184).

6. This concern is expressed by William Thompson in his introduction to *The Contemporary Novel in France*, p. 28.

7. Historiographic metafiction, in Linda Hutcheon's terms, is a "confrontation" in which "documentary historical actuality meets formalist self-reflexivity and parody" in both works of art and history (7).

8. In *After the Great Divide* (1986), Huyssen loosely defines the technological imagination as "artistic practices such as collage, assemblage, montage and photomontage; it finds its ultimate fulfillment in photography and film, art forms which can not only be reproduced, but are in fact designed for mechanical reproduction" (9). It should also be mentioned that in 1980, Huyssen served as co-editor of a book (alongside Teresa de Lauretis and Kathleen Woodward) entitled *The Technological Imagination: Theories and Fictions*, one of whose central premises is that "literary and artistic production, even when not strictly dependent on the development of special technical means, reflects that cultural transformation and the technologies that effect it" (viii). The editors make the additional point that research concerning the relationship between technology, literature, and culture has not been undertaken in any major way in literary studies. Their book nevertheless still remains one of the only full-scale contributions in this direction.

9. As Pierre Sorlin affirms, "There is no immunity against the media. Even people who never read a newspaper and have no television set are surrounded by messages, be it only advertisements stuck on walls, which they cannot ignore" (17).

10. Because my focus here is less the ideological implications of the media and more their social function, I refer the reader to Pierre Sorlin for a more lengthy discussion of this problematic.

11. Indeed, not only is *what* we know increasingly dependent on the power of the media, but, as Andreas Huyssen aptly describes, *how* we know as well: "The more memory we store on data banks, the more the past is sucked into the orbit of the present, ready to be called up on screen...As such simultaneity wipes out the alterity of past and present, here and there, it tends to lose its anchor in referentiality, in the real, and the present falls victim to its magical power of simulation and image projection...In the most extreme case, the boundaries between fact and fiction, reality and perception have been blurred to the extent that it leaves us with only simulation, and the postmodern subject vanishes in the imaginary world of the screen" (*Twilight Memories* 253–4).

12. As Pierre Sorlin maintains, "There is a creative side in any form of reception so that the experience and competence of the public, what we might call its media culture, has also to be taken into account. Deciphering the intended meaning or message conveyed by a paper or a poster implies some skill. The users have to learn the system of signs which, by social conventions, stand for a particular object or circumstance. The content of a newspaper article cannot be reduced to the substance of the words it contains" (84).

13. I borrow the term "social world" from Aviad Raz and Rina Shapira who use it "as a concept focusing on the unique role of a certain communication network from which emerges a distinct mode of social interaction.... The symbolic core of many social worlds is not human relationships per se but human relationships as revolving around a certain object, such as the computer, the painting, the liquor bottle, or 'the community' (416). For our purposes, this object is the screen.

14. Such changes, aptly described by Raz and Shapira, include the lack of "all the subtle clues (e.g. facial expressions, bodily gestures, the physical distance/proximity between interlocutors) that we generally look for when we are involved in face-to-face interaction" (413).

15. Umberto Eco makes a similar point in a different context. Speaking about the reading of books on CD/ROM which include a hyper-text function, he comments: "It is said that a story on CD/ROM may allow the reader to change the ending and induce characters to live through new vicissitudes. There are examples of works prepared in this way. But in this case, no new literature has replaced the one we have known for a few thousand years. A new literary type has been created, similar to what is called a jam session in jazz, when a composition is created based on improvisation. New forms do not supplant the old, which we continue to need very deeply" ("Why New Media Won't Kill Books" 17).

16. Here Guillaume's analysis can be read as an extension of Michel Foucault's work into the domain of media technology since he articulates spectrality as a particular form of an "ethics of the self" seeking to resist the disciplinary mechanisms of the society of normalization. In the carnival of spectres, regulatory principles such as 'truth' and the 'norm' have little currency. Participants may therefore strive for alternate modes of subjectivity that remain *transitory* ones. In this sense, spectrality may be viewed in terms of the "arts of the self" described by Foucault in the second volume of the *History of Sexuality* and in various articles and interviews concerning the "minimalist self" or the regimes of truth.

17. Such is the method outlined by Dick Hebdige concerning leftist politics: "A sociology of aspiration might begin by combining the considerable *critical* and *diagnostic* resources available within existing versions of sociology and cultural studies with the *descriptive* and *predictive* knowledge available within the new intensive market research to get a more adequate picture of what *everybody* says they want and what they want to be in all its radical plurality. The challenge would, then, be to produce and distribute the required goods and services more efficiently and equitably than the opposition. Such a mix…would take the Left beyond the ghetto of 'miserabilism' to which it is regularly consigned by the loony Right. Such a shift would require what certain forms of postmodernism recommend: a skepticism towards imposed general, 'rational' solutions; a relaxation of the old critical and judgmental postures although it emphatically does not necessitate a retreat from first principles and primary objectives: a commitment to social justice, equality of opportunity and social welfare" (232).

18. See Brian McHale's *Postmodernist Fiction*, pp. 197–232.

19. It is important to note the importance of Blanchot's thought to postmodernism. Both John Gregg and Brian McHale qualify Blanchot as a postmodernist, and Gregg presents a thorough analysis of the impact of Blanchot's theories of representation on postmodern thinkers such as Baudrillard and Deleuze to name only two examples. See John Gregg's *Maurice Blanchot and the Literature of Transgression*, pp. 173–200.

20. As Gregg explains, Baudrillard's remarks on simulation and simulacra can be read as an adaptation of the theory of the simulacrum as it is found in Blanchot. There are nevertheless important differences insofar as power is concerned, which Gregg summarizes in the following passage: "In his theorization of the hyperreal, Baudrillard appears to take Blanchot furthur than Blanchot himself would probably like by imagining a world that Sorge, Blanchot, and Bataille would never even have dreamed of, one in which simulacra and *ressemblance* are the order of the day and where the regional economy of power is *truly* regional, a caricature of its former self…. Whereas the philosophers of difference can still engage themselves in the subversion of totalizing systems through a Nietzschean affirmation of heterogeneity, Baudrillard no longer allows himself this attitude, which must appear to him as a luxury" (188).

21. In his article entitled "On Fascination: Walter Benjamin's Images," Ackbar Abbas reminds us that fascination, although not normally associated with critical thought, can be used as a critical tool. In his words, "We are reminded

time and again that in the allure of fascination lies a lure. Perhaps it is because of this ambivalence that when fascination is involved in cultural and political theory, it is most often disparaged as a state of illusion and passivity, characterized by the loss or suspension of the critical faculties.... Benjaminian method [and Blanchotian, we would add] gives fascination itself a critical role. He sees in fascination not a will-less affect, not the response of last resort, but a willingness to be drawn to phenomena that attract our attention yet do not submit entirely to our understanding. Benjamin works out a method sensitive to an ambiguous and complex situation, a method which in practice consists of patiently entrusting thought to the folds of the image" (51). This method is also present in the texts of Genet, Guibert, and Bouraoui.

22. In the *The Use of Pleasure: The History of Sexuality, Vol II* Foucault defines these "arts of existence" or "techniques of the self" as "those intentional and voluntary actions by which men not only set themselves rules of conduct, but also *seek to transform themselves, to change themselves in their singular being, and to make their life into an* oeuvre *that carries certain aesthetic values and meets certain stylistic criteria*" (10–11, my emphasis). This definition approximates what Blanchot discusses in relation to the writer's approach to the space of literature. In both cases, the voluntary submission to, and work on, limits through transgression is an integral component to both theorists' conception of subjectivity. For studies that explore transgression and subjectivity in the work of Blanchot and Foucault, see John Gregg's *Maurice Blanchot and the Literature of Trangression*, and Jon Simon's *Foucault and the Political*, as well as Foucault's study on Blanchot, "La Pensée du dehors," and Blanchot's study on Foucault, "Foucault tel que je l'imagine."

23. For pertinent discussions on subjectivity and cyberspace, see Giuseppe Mantovani's "Virtual Reality as a Communication Environment: Consensual Hallucination, Fiction, and Possible Selves," and Sherry Turkle's "Constructions and Reconstructions of Self in Virtual Reality: Playing in the MUDs."

2 | "La Glorification de l'Image et du Reflet" or The Mediatization of Identity, History, and Nationalism in Jean Genet

La gloire, c'est rester un, et se prostituer d'une manière particulière.
Glorifier le culte des images (ma grande, mon unique, ma primitive passion)
— *Baudelaire*

In his preface to *Le Balcon* (1956), Jean Genet explicitly articulates a mode of representation that is pivotal to his entire literary and artistic *oeuvre*: "la glorification de l'Image et du Reflet" (12). Finding its most direct expression in the mirror—a device that has become a hallmark of sorts for Genet who never fails to evoke its reflective powers of fascination—the interplay of images and their doubles ("reflets" or shadows) as well as the subversion of conventional notions of the real(istic) and a privileging of artifice have proven to be the most salient features of Genet's artistic creation, especially his theater.

For this reason, critics generally maintain that theatricality— understood here as performativity, performance rites and rituals, and metamorphosis in play acting—is the most important dimension of Genet's *oeuvre*, particularly insofar as it relates to the construction of subjectivity and identity formation.[1] Although criticism on Genet has effectively underscored the primary mechanisms in his texts that contribute to highlighting the formation of the subject in a performative mode (such as the mirror, photographs, and patronyms, etc.), there is a tendency to reduce this central element of Genet's work to either strictly personal or purely aesthetic motivations. Gene Plunka writes, for example, that "[t]o understand the logic behind Genet's distorted syllogisms, one must first come to grips with his premise. At the core of Genet's writing is a firm belief that he is an outcast, a marginal man, and as such, he vents his anger and frustration at a society that defined him as 'marginal'" (36). Laura Oswald ascribes a similar function to Genet's artistic endeavors and aesthetic when she proposes that "Jean Genet's life as a writer inhabited his life as an outcast, a prisoner, and a homosexual. Speaking from the margins of dominant culture, Genet attempted throughout his career to represent the silent side of proper bourgeois culture and history, celebrating crime, sedition, and sexual perversion in a style that tested the limits of the French language" ("Middle East Voices" 46).

Arguments of this sort are certainly plausible since Genet provides ample evidence of his indifference, if not hatred, toward most forms of sociality and government, as well as of his marginal status in French society as an illegitimate child and, later, as a petty thief. A passage from an interview with Hubert Fichte illustrates this by-now famous posture on the part of Genet. When asked to give a personal definition of political revolution, Genet responds,

> Non, parce que je ne tiens pas tellement à ce qu'il y ait une révolution. Si je suis sincère, je n'y tiens pas. La situation actuelle, les régimes actuels me permettent la révolte, mais la révolution ne me permettrait probablement pas la révolte, c'est-à-dire de la révolte individuelle. Mais ce régime me permet la révolte individuelle. Je peux être contre lui. Mais, s'il s'agissait d'une véritable révolution, je ne pourrais peut-être pas être contre. Il y aurait adhésion et l'homme que je suis n'est pas un homme d'adhésion, c'est un homme de révolte. Mon point de vue est très égoïste. Je voudrais que le monde, mais faites bien attention à la façon dont je le dis, je voudrais que le monde ne change pas, pour me permettre d'être contre le monde. (*Dialogues* 25)

It is undeniable that had Genet not experienced life on the margins of society, prostituting himself, stealing, and living in the streets, he might have developed an altogether different perspective on dominant cultural structures and institutions and the role of identity therein. To assume, however, that this experience is *predominantly* responsible for his artistic aesthetic is in my view to fall prey to the Genet mystique, which began with the publication of Sartre's *Saint Genet: Comédien et Martyr* (1963) and which continues still today.[2]

If theoretical and critical approaches to Genet have often filtered the emphasis on performativity and theatricality in his work through his social status and personal ethics, there are those who see this dimension of Genet in purely formalist terms. Bernard Dort, one of the leading scholars on Genet's dramatic works, maintains, for example, that Genet's aesthetic of artifice serves a principally self-reflexive function—a celebration of theater (or representation as is the case in Genet's novels) only to better destroy it: "Genet's theater is, in the literal sense of the word, a theater of representation: not only a theater within the theater, but also theater about the theater. A doubly theatrical theater" (123). Certainly, Genet's work constitutes in itself a critique of traditional realist representation on the one hand.[3] Yet to assert that it contains no profound sociological or political reflections on the other, as many do (including Genet), is no more convincing than critiques based primarily on Genet's existential position as an outcast struggling to be heard.[4]

What, we may ask, does account then for Genet's specifically "theatrical" vision of society and representation if not the above elements? Given Genet's painstaking attention to the multiple functions of the image and the powers of fascination it exercises over perception of reality (whether it be personal, political, or artistic), I suggest that image technologies can be pinpointed as major factors in the development of Genet's artistic corpus. In effect, Genet's interest in the power of the image and reflection extends beyond questions of the social construction of subjectivity, the desire to assault bourgeois social morality, or strictly formalist practices. The overwhelming presence of images springing from the pages of newspapers, magazines, posters, film, radio and popular French serials in Genet's texts indicates, in line with Walter Benjamin's theories, a broader shift in the writing process itself and even in the literary imagination, and calls for a reevaluation not only of the interplay between reality and fiction in Genet, but also of subjectivity and death in his work.

To this end, I propose an approach in this chapter that shifts the focus of Genet's treatment of subjectivity and identity away from his marginalized position in society. Rather, by focusing on the impact of media technologies, I will investigate the extent to which Genet's conception of the image accounts for the fragmentary subjectivity, shifting identity, and simulacrum effect particular to his work. While this problematic bears on Genet's entire corpus, I have chosen to concentrate specifically on only two works due to their treatment of historical events: *Pompes funèbres* (1947) and *Les Paravents* (1961).

The justification for this kind of an approach inscribes itself not only in the creative texts themselves, but also in the need to rethink the relationship between technology, the imagination, and literature. Indeed, postmodernist fiction, in its overt exploitation of media technologies such as television and cinema, is demonstrating more and more that "we must begin to understand technology as a relation of the technical and the cultural, as a material and cognitive form of social process" (de Lauretis et al., viii).[5]

Genet's aesthetic, through its marked attention to the mechanically reproduced image, is testimony to the fact that image culture shapes the very content and form of the imagination in our time. Genet himself draws attention to this phenomenon when he makes the following remarks to Hubert Fichte concerning the importance of his work in the socio-political sphere. Reacting to what he sees as Fichte's exaggeration of the significance of his work, Genet responds:

> Même si mes livres ont eu un certain retentissement, l'acte d'écrire, l'acte singulier d'écrire dans une prison ne m'a presque pas affecté, de sorte qu'il y a une disproportion entre ce que vous me décrivez qui serait le résultat obtenu par mes livres et l'écriture de mes livres.... Je me demande s'il n'y a pas un phénomène de grossissement qui est dû aux moyens de transmission et de reproduction mécaniques. Il y a 200 ans, si un homme avait fait mon portrait il y aurait eu un portrait. Maintenant, si on fait une photographie de moi - on en tire 200 000, même davantage, bon, mais est-ce que j'ai plus d'importance? (*Dialogues* 15)

The "phénomène de grossissement" linked to mechanical reproduction and evoked here by Genet in relation to his own image is evident in both *Les Paravents* and *Pompes funèbres*, texts which take up and rework the officially sanctioned discourses surrounding two of France's most controversial moments in history: the Algerian War and World War II. Throughout this chapter we will see that if image technologies in these texts are represented as tools which aid in the production of a homogenous and rationalized national "truth" on the one hand, they nevertheless open up a space for negotiation with and resistence to dominant cultural images through death and fascination on the other. Before turning to *Pompes funèbres* and *Les Paravents* specifically, however, let us first take a closer look at media technologies in Genet's novels on a general level so that we may better understand not only their centrality to his elaboration of the literary imagination, but also their connection to the fragmentation and disintegration of the subject and fixed identity.

Media Images and Visual Fascination in Genet

In chapter one, we discussed the capacity of media technologies to significantly alter our sense of space and time—the local and the global—contributing to a "flattening" of experience and "robbing us," as John Tomlinson puts it, "of the differentiations that give events particular significances" (60). "Cultural amnesia," the mythification of history, the expulsion of death from the social sphere, and the more recent shift toward globalization are some elements commonly presumed to be linked to the ubiquitous presence of media in our lives.[6]

We also saw, however, that images themselves, through their radically weightless, "cadaverous" presence and powers of fascination, open up spaces of negotiation wherein audiences may divert the messages received by the media to their own uses, pleasures and desires, and, at the same time, refashion their identities. In this sense, as Ella Shohat and Robert Stam suggest, while the media play a role in shaping identity along the lines of dominant cultural formations such as Eurocentrism or consumer culture, they nevertheless cannot be separated "from the desire, experience, and knowledge of historically situated spectators, constituted outside the text and traversed by sets of power relations such as nation, race, class, gender, and sexuality" (347). In other words, while media images help to shape the way "we" see ourselves and thus are implicated in the construction of our subjectivity and identity, our lived experience, in turn, shapes the way "we" receive the media.

The contamination and alteration of lived experience, subjectivity, and identity by (media) technologies is commonly foregrounded in postmodernist writing, and can be found similarly at work throughout Jean Genet's texts. Throughout his novels *Miracle de la rose* (1946), *Notre-Dame-des-fleurs* (1948), *Journal du voleur* (1949), *Pompes funèbres* (1952), *Querelle de Brest* (1953), and *Un Captif amoureux* (1986), for example, information and images gathered from newspapers, popular songs, pulp fiction, magazines, and cinema are mixed with highly personalized narratives that are supposedly written from Genet's own life experiences.[7] An example from *Miracle de la rose* illustrates the extent to which the diagesis, written in the first person, is effected by the experience of technology, especially (mechanically reproduced) images. In recollecting his "incestuous" love for a fellow inmate Divers (a point I will return to below), the author-narrator's memories become confused with the emotions he experienced while cutting out the image of a famous criminal, Pilorge, from a popular police serial. As a result of the seductive powers of the image, the subject slips into the image and, in doing so, experiences an *évanouissement* or fading of himself. This loss of subjectivity, in turn, entails a further destabilization: a blurring of the lines between what is presented as reality (Divers's face), and its facsimile (the photographic image of Pilorge):

> Le visage de Divers était moins méchant qu'étrange. Ce n'est qu'en l'embrassant que je le reconnais un peu, qu'il me semblait le voir se présenter sous un aspect nouveau et troublant, ouvrant des perspectives inconnues. J'éprouvai cette émotion lorsque je découpai, dans un journal policier, la photographie de Pilorge. Mes ciseaux suivaient lentement la ligne du visage et cette lenteur m'obligeait à distinguer les détails, le grain de la peau, l'ombre du nez sur la joue. D'un point de vue neuf, j'apercevais ce visage chéri. Puis, devant le tourner de haut en bas pour les facilités du découpage, *il me composa soudain* un paysage montagneux, d'un relief lunaire, plus désert et désolé qu'un paysage du Tibet. J'avançais sur la ligne du front, je tournais un peu et *soudain, avec la rapidité d'une locomotive emballée, fonçaient sur moi* des perspectives d'ombres, des gouffres de douleur.... *J'étais abandonné* dans une gorge ou sur un pic, saisi par la découverte d'un visage d'assassin. (256, my emphasis)

In the narrator's contemplation of—and identification with—the image, Divers's face becomes indistinguishable from Pilorge's, making it impossible to tell the original (or "true-life") character from the model (his photographic double).[8] Images here become contagious, proliferating amongst themselves to reproduce only more images or, in other words, doubles, hence the "incestuous" nature of the author-narrator's love and his inevitable—albeit momentary—transformation into an image in his own right. Drawn irresistably into the image—a movement that alters the subject's mastery over reality—the author-narrator, as in Guillaume's model of spectrality, is doubly dispossessed of himself. He undergoes a loss of subjectivity, and is placed into a state of utter passivity while the image takes on an active role. First, the image composes not only new surroundings for the author-narrator (a sort of virtual reality *avant la lettre*), but it also composes the narrator himself ("il me composa"). Then, with the speed of a locomotive (like the first cinematic images), the image overtakes the narrator, propulsing him into a shadowy (erotic/masochistic) realm of physical pain. Within this movement, the "I" of the narrator is literally abandoned—"J[e] étais abandonné"—and he becomes part of the tableau created by the image of Pilorge. In this sense, images stemming from a variety of sources lead, as Jerry Aline Flieger remarks in another context, "to an interplay of proliferated images, in which every [image] is fair game to be used in engendering another, and in which time and space may be telescoped at will. This imagistic proliferation results in the consistently overdetermined character of Genet's text[s], contributing to the overall oneiric cast of the work" (73).[9]

Images of notorious criminals clipped from newpapers and magazines, a leitmotif in Genet's novels, are therefore less archetypes or symbols deployed solely for the purposes of Genet's erotic and/or criminal imaginary. Rather, in their capacity to contaminate and modulate the real, drawing the author-narrator into a space of fascination (the space of the screen) where subjective stability is undermined and his relation to the real is subsequently altered, images in Genet's texts function as simulacra: Blanchotian cadaverous presences or spectres in Guillaume's sense that seize their spectator and propulse him into a realm where "'Je' ne 'se' reconnaît pas" (*L'Espace littéraire* 357). As Blanchot further describes,

> Vivre un événement en image, ce n'est pas se dégager de cet événement, s'en désintéresser, comme le voudraient la version esthétique de l'image et l'idéal serein de l'art classique, mais ce n'est non plus s'y engager par une décision libre: *c'est s'y laisser prendre, passer de la région du réel, où nous nous tenons à distance des choses pour mieux en disposer, à cet autre région où la distance nous tient.*... Intime est l'image, parce qu'elle fait de notre intimité une puissance extérieure que nous subissons passivement: en dehors de nous, dans le recul du monde qu'elle provoque, traîne, égarée et brillante, la profondeur de nos passions. (*Espace* 352, my emphasis)

In Genet's texts, the experience of living an event *in* image described here by Blanchot is transposed into writing through what could be called, following Steven Shaviro, a predominantly cinematic gaze.[10] Shaviro, going against the grain of conventional psychoanalytic film theory, which generally aligns the subject's gaze with a position of mastery and control, argues for a model of cinematic spectatorship based primarily on the experience of self-abandonment.[11] Drawing on Benjamin's analysis of shock, Michael Taussig's work on the mimetic faculty, and Blanchot's theory of the image, Shaviro demonstrates that cinematic spectatorship, far from stabilizing the subject through processes of identification, is first and foremost a destabilizing, tactile, and visceral experience:

> Cinema produces real effects *in* the viewer, rather than merely presenting phantasmatic reflections *to* the viewer. The cinematic image is not an object for some (actual or ideal) spectator; instead, the spectator is drawn into the fragmented materiality and the 'depth without depth' of the image. *I am solicited and invested by what I see: perception becomes a kind of physical affliction, an intensification and disarticulation of bodily sensation*, rather than a process of naive (ideological and Imaginary) belief or of detached, attentive consideration. (52, my emphasis)

Significantly, according to Shaviro, within this realm of "tactile convergences" of images, the subject is driven not by a desire for "possession, plenitude, stability, and reassurance" (54). Rather, in its confrontation with images, the subject enters into a space of liminality and intoxication that inevitably leads to *disempowerment*. Indeed, this space dissolves the contours of the ego and transgresses the requirements of coherence and closure that govern 'normal' experience. In this new realm, the gaze is at once fascinated and distracted, but in any case passive and not possessive. The world of static, stabilizing self-representations slips out from under me. I am drawn instead into a realm of Heraclitean flux, a time and space from which all fixed points of reference and self-reference, all lines of perspective, and all possibilities of stabilizing identification and objectification are banished. (Shaviro 54)

This is precisely the realm that is opened in the encounter between the gaze and the image in Genet's texts. Querelle's first visit to La Féria, the whorehouse in Genet's *Querelle de Brest*, for instance, aptly illustrates the destabilizing effects of visual fascination so convincingly analyzed by Shaviro. Upon entering La Féria, a fantastic place shrouded in mystery and situated outside time and space (much like the realm of the cinematic image in Shaviro's description),[12] Querelle encounters Mario, a police officer, and Norbert, the owner of the whorehouse, who appear as images from a film noir. The mechanical nature of the reproduction of these two characters is emphasized not only by the presence of the mirror, which here serves as the physical presence of the movie screen, but also by the fact that although he is facing Mario and Norbert, Querelle is presented as *looking up* at the two men whose images blur together under his gaze in an endless process of doubling. Querelle, like the cinematic spectator, is thus plunged into a space where he loses touch with himself, becoming "transfixed and transmogrified in consequence of the infectious, visceral contact of images" (Shaviro 53).

Mario était immobile, presque absent. Il était debout contre le comptoir et derrière lui la glace réfléchissait son dos. Sans dire un mot, il se détacha de cet accoudoir qui lui permettait une pose intéressante, et il vint s'adosser au miroir, près du patron: *il parut s'appuyer à soi-même.* En face des deux hommes Querelle éprouva tout à coup un malaise, une sorte d'écoeurement comme en connaissent les assassins. Le calme et la beauté de Mario le déconcertaient. Ils étaient trop grands. Le patron du bordel— Norbert—était trop fort. Mario aussi. Les lignes du corps de l'un allaient à l'autre, une confusion terrible mêlait les deux musculatures, les deux visages.... *A l'intérieur de soi, Querelle sentit trembler, vaciller, sur le point de s'abolir dans un vomissement, ce qui était proprement lui-même. Saisi de vertige devant*

cette puissance de chair et de nerfs qu'il apercevait très haute—en levant la tête comme
on voudrait toiser un sapin géant—qui se doublait et se dédoublait constamment....
Querelle gardait la bouche un peu entr'ouverte, le palais un peu sec.
(31–32, my emphasis)

Querelle's encounter with the cinematic image, as it moves him to a point outside of himself (a point represented here as an abolishment of self), renders him effectively powerless. Critics who have specifically treated the function of images and media in Genet's work largely overlook this process of self-annihilation undergone by protagonists in front of images, an element which nevertheless remains a constant throughout Genet's novels, theatre, and even his more "political" and theoretical writings, thus establishing a certain (but by no means inclusive) continuity not only between his works, but also in his theory of the image itself. For the most part, critics have focused instead on Genet's use of the media and popular culture images as tools toward either personal or aesthetic ends. The general lines of the argument are as follows: Genet, the homosexual, criminal poet, appropriates social and political discourses from the newspapers as well as clichéd images from pulp fiction stories or mainstream film in order to show up the hypocrisy of bourgeois socio-cultural norms.[13] Media images from this perspective function only as superficial props for Genet's own fantasies (thus explaining the hallucinatory or dream-like context of his work), subordinated as it were to deeper purposes specific to his own (poetic/erotic) aesthetic such as the elaboration of an ethics of betrayal and the glorification of evil or even outright narcissism. More than thirty years ago, Jean-Paul Sartre had drawn such conclusions:

> The origins of these plots are the stories which Genet read in prison: as we have seen, he draws his original inspiration from the most popular sources; he has assimilated the poetry of the adventure story as well as that of music-hall songs.... The wax dummy that was found by the detective in Our Lady's room recalls the blood-stained dolls of Fantomas. Genet borrows the paraphernalia of the adventure stories partly out of fidelity to the prisoner that he was, partly to pull the leg of the bourgeois intellectual by making him swallow the cock-and-bull story that he claims to despise, but mainly because he wants his works to have a 'taste of

fiction'.... All these fictional props are present in order to be suddenly sacrificed to Genet himself. (522)

The visual fascination to which Genet's protagonists succumb, however, presents a much more suggestive and complex relationship to these mass marketed images, and complicates arguments based primarily on the author-narrator's *active* and *willful* mode of appropriation of images. For indeed, as we discussed above, in Genet's highly artificial universe images overtake their spectator, luring him into a state of passivity and placing him into a position of exteriority where literally he is separated from himself (a symbolic death which, following Blanchot and Guillaume, is also the space of the screen and of literature). Images in this sense represent less the solidification of the self into an essence or a projection of the author's omnipotence through the realization of his fantasies, as many critics advance. Rather, as we will see, the self achieves permanence through the image in Genet only as a form of relationality with *death*, that is to say a way of symbolically exchanging with the dead. By fusing with the image, much like in cyberspace, the subject loses any notion of fixed identity (the self is in fact annihilated and copied into another, transformed into a spectral subject), and instead takes on the characteristics that define the image itself, namely, in Genet's case, an erotic power and connection to death.[14] Images can thus be said to structure Genet's narratives[15] first by provoking fascination in the viewer (author/character/narrator) and, subsequently, by distancing him from the "world of reality" (thereby contextualizing the constant interplay of reality and fiction typical to Genet's work).[16]

Querelle's transformation from a simple assassin to a seductive image amply illustrates the doubling of the subject that occurs in its encounter with the image, as well as culture's commodification of military (male) power as sexual power, one of whose most impressive icons is a man in uniform.[17] In the following example, the sailor's uniform serves as the screen which at once mediates the stereotypical image of the ideal sailor and creates the space necessary for the split in the subject to occur:

Querelle éprouvait obscurément d'être sur le point de toucher à sa perfection: sous son costume admirable dont le prestige fabuleux le recouvrait, il n'était plus seulement le simple assassin mais encore le séducteur…. Querelle se fortifiait donc encore de toute la force de la Marine de guerre. *Semblant courir après sa propre forme, à chaque instant l'atteindre et cependant la poursuivre* il marchait vite, sûr de lui, le pied bien posé. Son corps s'armait de canons, de coques d'acier, de torpilles, d'un équipage agile et lourd, belliqueux et précis. Querelle devenait 'le Querelle', destroyer géant, écumeur de mer, masse métallique intelligente et butée. (33)

There is no stable subject position in Genet's texts ("Querelle devenait 'le Querelle'"); there are only commodified images of such stability and these images, to a large extent, engender the doublings and reflections so characteristic of Genet's ornate visual tableaux. Within these tableaux, as Steven Shaviro remarks about Fassbinder's filmic adaptation of *Querelle*—a description that also applies to Genet's texts—"[w]e quickly come to recognize the play of simulacra: since everything…is a reflection, an 'imitation of life,' 'reality' and 'life' are entirely exhausted and consumed by artifice, or by commodification" (167) leaving in their place only theatrical enactments of power or, as Genet puts it in *Le Balcon*, the outright "glorification de l'Image et du Reflet."

History as Simulation and the "Death of the Subject"

I began my inquiry into Genet's theory of the image through an exploration of the transformations media technologies have operated in the literary imagination. More specifically, I treated the problematic of subjectivity, and showed that for Genet, the space of the screen is a space where subjects project themselves into images (themselves generated in large part by the author-narrator's use of media and popular culture imagery) and thus experience a symbolic death which, in turn, leads to new identities and subjectivities. In some cases, as we saw with Querelle, subjects readily identify with the cultural codification of the image and thus assume its "subject effects" wholeheartedly. In other cases, however, identification with the image can lead the subject to reject its cultural context and, in so doing, produce "aberrant" readings that open the image to negotiation. "What interests Genet," then, as Leo Bersani has argued, "is not the way society distributes predicaments but rather the way it assigns identities. It is the taking on—or attempted refusal—of those identities that determines the possibility of effective rebellion" (14). Identity in this sense is much less a matter of essentializing existence for Genet; rather, identity exists only in simulation.

The question of media and simulated identities has been posed in contemporary discourses from a variety of perspectives. On the one hand, in discourses on cyberspace and virtual reality, the death of the subject opens largely onto a space of freedom and choice. "In this accommodating reality," writes Kevin Robins, "the self is reconstituted as a fluid and polymorphous entity. Identities can be selected or discarded almost at will, as in a game or a fiction" (88). On the other hand, in sociological and political discourses, the loss of fixed identity is not necessarily a liberating (utopian) experience, but rather an experience of *loss*—the loss of control over (social and historical) reality: "We now articulate our identity through coming to terms with the image rather than the reality. The system of images, apparently self-contained and auto-referential, comes to assume its own autonomy and authority" (Robins 44). Within the domain of cultural studies and postcolonial discourses, the question of the death of the subject and identity formation has been posed with even more urgency, crystallizing in what could be called the "PC phenomenon:"

> Today's PC is associated with a political atmosphere dominated by identity politics and issues of self-representation, issues fraught with personal and political tensions about who speaks, when, how, and in whose name. The politics of identity call for the 'self-representation' of marginalized communities, for 'speaking for oneself.' And while poststructuralist feminist, gay/lesbian, and postcolonial theories have often rejected essentialist articulations of identity, and biologistic and transhistorical determinations of gender, race, and sexual orientation, they have at the same time supported 'affirmative action' politics, implicitly premised on the very categories elsewhere rejected as essentialist, leading to a paradoxical situation where theory deconstructs totalizing myths while activism nourishes them. Theory and practice, then, seem to pull in apparently opposite directions. (Shohat and Stam 342)

Genet's presentation of the interface between (media) images and identity is highly relevant to these problematics, and especially to the construction of alternative subjectivities, for no other author of the twentieth century has so directly confronted and staged, in all its dimensions, one of the most pressing critical issues of postmodern times: how to articulate the struggle to become subjects of history in an era of the "death of the subject."[18] Or, to put it another way, on what ground is resistance to be negotiated in an era where the language of revolution has been largely eclipsed, and the decentering of identities comes close to paralyzing group efforts to mobilize toward shared emancipatory goals?

For Genet, as for many artists, theorists, and writers of the postmodern period, image technologies play a significant part in the shaping of identities and subjectivities on both a local (personal) and a global (national/historical) scale. As the Queen's messenger remarks in *Le Balcon* after having witnessed an orchestrated photo session of the newly inaugurated power figures (who, in "reality," are clients of Irma's whorehouse simulating the identities of Judges, Archbishops, and Generals), "Ce qui compte, c'est la lecture ou l'Image. L'Histoire fut vécue afin qu'une page glorieuse soit écrite puis lue" (123). History is presented here as no more than a mere simulation enacted to support the dominant, Eurocentric view of civilization, and revolution in this scenario must necessarily follow suit, for as Roger, the leader of the revolutionaries, understands only too well: "La lutte ne se passe plus dans la réalité, mais en champ clos. Sur champ d'azur. C'est le combat des allégories. Ni les uns ni les autres nous ne voyons plus les raisons de notre révolte" (*Le Balcon* 95).

Roger's description of the eclipse of a political and historical consciousness situates such loss within an image culture that, by force of combating image-allegories, induces not an ever-clearer vision but blindness. This condition finds an echo in contemporary image culture wherein, as Robins explains, the screen "presents us with a wealth of information, but equally it functions to screen out the reality of what is seen and to inhibit knowledge" (117). In texts where Genet brings war and colonialism into focus—*Pompes funèbres, Le Balcon, Les Nègres, Les Paravents,* and *Un Captif amoureux*—similar appraisals of the discrepancy between the seer and what is seen (experienced) are presented through Genet's vision of history as simulation. In these texts, Genet engages in strategies typical to the postmodernist revisionist historical novel, whereby he juxtaposes the officially-accepted version of historical events with another, often radically dissimilar version of the world.[19] Significantly, Genet often draws on mass media images to perform this disjunction.

What I will address throughout the remainder of this chapter are the ways in which Genet deploys image technologies to develop an "anti-Eurocentric" vision of history, a vision which heightens awareness of all the cultural voices at play in the making of history (especially those of the dead), and where spectatorship, rather than constituting a passive act of self-indulgence, becomes an act of self-confrontation.

Images of (La) Résistance: *Pompes funèbres*

Pompes funèbres, Genet's third novel, is written in an autobiographical mode; it recounts Genet's experience of the death and burial of his lover Jean Décarnin, a communist fighting in the Resistance and killed at the hands of a collaborator on the barricades less than a week before the liberation of Paris. The context of the German occupation of France during World War II is introduced to us in the opening paragraph of the novel, which begins with a graphic image of the effects of war described to us by the narrator who encounters it in the newspapers: "Les journaux qui parurent à la Libération de Paris, en août 1944, dirent assez ce que furent ces journées d'héroïsme puéril.... Des photographies montrent encore des cadavres dépecés, mutilés et des villages en ruines, Ouradour et Montsauche incendiés par les soldats allemands" (7). This image, far from containing any shock value or provoking a sense of moral outrage, is all too familiar to readers living in the postmodern period. By the sheer force of exposure to multiple images of death that circulate on a daily basis, we have become anaesthetized to the effects of such violence. As Kevin Robins points to, "[t]hrough the distancing force of images, frozen registrations of remote calamities, we have learned to manage our relationship with suffering" (77). Images thus have the capacity to de-realize death, altering in the process not only our relationship to the dead, but also our experience of death. Indeed, as Robins argues, in terms that resonate with Baudrillard's and Blanchot's theorization of Western culture's attitude toward death, the consumption of the media's "pornography of dying" can be understood as culture's effort to eradicate death in the interest of gaining power and mastery over it.

The narrative of *Pompes funèbres* attempts to counterbalance the distancing effect of media images through its telling of the story of Jean D.'s death. In recounting memories of Jean, however, a displacement of lived experience (the extremely personal experience of a lover's death) by mediated experience (its representation in newspapers, political propaganda and cinema) is constantly put into motion and the narrator's story, far from bringing us any closer to the circumstances of Jean's death, instead offers the reader a series of narrative fragments wherein Nazism, the French Résistance and the close of World War II provide real-life historical backdrops to an otherwise fantastical tale of love, death, and betrayal.

Significantly, as we saw above, media images—the newspaper photographs of mutilated bodies tortured and burned by German soldiers of the opening paragraph of the novel—serve as the primary vehicles by which the narrator brings historical reality into focus in *Pompes funèbres*. At the same time, however, these images also enable the narrator to establish an alternating principle between "reality" (the war, Jean's death) and "fiction" (Hitler, in fact, becomes a character/narrator in the novel). Through this process, not only is the reliability of official history questioned. The mythologizing components (e.g. *staged* rituals such as media events) prevalent in all forms of nationalism, whether they be on the Left (communist) or on the Right (fascist), are also scrutinized.

In *Pompes funèbres*, the alternating principle between "reality" and "fiction" is enacted by the narrator's presentation of Jean's death and burial through the double lens of the media and memory. The opening lines of the novel conjure up simultaneously the memory of the last days of the war when Jean was killed, as well as its staging in the newspaper headlines of the time:

> 'Paris vivant!' 'Parisiens, tous dans la rue!' 'L'Armée américaine défile dans Paris.' 'Les combats dans les rues continuent.' 'Les Boches ont capitulé.' 'Aux barricades!', 'A mort les traîtres!'.... En compulsant les vieilles

feuilles nous revoyons les visages durcis et souriants, gris de la poussière des rues, de la fatigue, d'une barbe de quatre ou cinq jours. Peu de temps après ces journaux rappelleront les massacres hitlériens, les jeux que d'autres appellent sadiques, d'une police qui recrutait ses plus terribles tortionnaires parmi les Français.... C'est à l'intérieur de cette tragédie que se place l'événement: la mort de Jean D. qui donne prétexte à ce livre. (7–8)

In quoting these particular headlines, Genet is going beyond the mere citation of news events. Indeed, by inscribing his story within the framework of mass media ("à l'intérieur de cette tragédie"—a term that refers ambiguously to both the historical and the theatrical/artificial), Genet effectively underscores the constructed and staged dimensions not only of the French Resistance, but also, and perhaps more importantly, of national history. More specifically, and this is where mass media images go beyond mere thematics to become structuring agents of the text itself, these images demonstrate that for Genet, as for Benedict Anderson, "[t]he 'style' of imagining nation-ness is essentially a mass mediated style, one achieved in literate societies with well-developed communication structures. It is an imagination encouraged by reading the national newspapers" (qtd. in Tomlinson 82).

In his work, Genet frequently addresses nationalist (imperialist) attempts to overwrite events and replace them with a homogenous vision that neatly falls in line with established national history. In *Pompes funèbres*, this attempt manifests itself through the mass media images cited above which, upon analysis, occult the fact that "sympathy to Nazism was higher in France before the start of the war than in any of the nations later occupied by Hitler, and [that] France democratically voted for Vichyism in 1940" (Grenier 46). The headlines quoted by Genet, which begin with "Paris vivant" and end with "A mort les traîtres," instead place emphasis on the "splendid myth," as Richard Grenier puts it, of a "France, defeated on the battlefield but unbowed in spirit," that "fought magnificently in the Résistance against the Nazi beast and played a major role in its own liberation" (46).

This mythologizing dimension of "national imagining" is echoed in two other scenes of primary importance in the novel, each involving the double lens of media and memory. The scenes I am referring to involve the narrator's witnessing of an "hommage populaire" in honor of Jean D. at the site of his death, a scene which in fact echoes the more formal burial—the *pompes funèbres* of the title—accorded to Jean by the State. In each ceremony, the appropriation of Jean's death toward the construction of a glorious national myth (to which we are introduced by the mass media at the opening of the novel) is accompanied by images of cannibalism. During the formal ceremony held for Jean in the church, when the priest pronounces the words "...Il est mort au champ d'honneur. Il est mort en luttant contre l'envahisseur" (27), the author-narrator imagines a burial altogether different:

> j'eusse pu porter son corps, et pourquoi les pouvoirs publics ne l'accordent-ils pas? le découper en morceaux dans une cuisine et le manger. Certes, il resterait beaucoup de déchets: les intestins, le foie, les poumons, surtout les yeux avec leurs paupières bordées de cils, que je ferais sécher et brûler, me réservant d'en mélanger les cendres à mes aliments, mais la chair pourrait s'assimiler à la mienne... (27)

The cannibalistic urge expressed here by the narrator in terms of a desire to ingest Jean so as to assimilate him out of love and grief for him returns during the popular homage, yet this time cannibalism is presented under a much more sinister light: the suspicion that ordinary French citizens (i.e. those not *explicitly* collaborating with the German regime) were equal to those referred to in the opening of the novel as participating in "les massacres hitlériens, les jeux que d'autres appellent sadiques" (7). This association is made when the narrator, in trying to find the site where Jean was killed, informs us that it is located near a small neighborhood "charcuterie." The narrator's cannibalistic urges to assimilate his lover's flesh in order to transform himself into a living memorial cited in the first passage here take on a completely different allure, that of collaboration:

> Je ne connaissais pas la saveur de la chair humaine, mais j'étais sûr de trouver à toutes saucisses et pâtés, un goût de cadavre. Le monde est d'accord. Je vis, effroyablement seul, désespéré, dans une société vorace qui protège une famille de charcutiers (le père, la mère, et trois gamins, sans doute) criminels, dépeceurs de cadavres, nourrissant la France entière

de jeunes morts, et qui se cache dans les profondeurs d'une boutique de
l'avenue Parmentier. (39)

Recalling here the "cadavres dépecés, mutilés" from the photographic
image of the opening pages of the novel, Genet is subtly interweaving both
the discourses of the media and those of memory into a cannibalistic
discourse of mourning and demystification: by ingesting Jean and becoming
his grave, the author-narrator creates a space of *symbolic exchange* with the
dead (indeed, he becomes the dead soldier, and speaks in his place),[20] a
space which will be associated neither with the nourishment of France and
its national myths (a space associated on one level with the screen), nor
even with its land (the most typical marker of national ties and a source of
key patriotic values for the Resistance):

> Aujourd'hui, je me fais horreur de contenir, l'ayant dévoré, le plus cher, le
> seul amant qui m'aimât. *Je suis son tombeau. La terre n'est rien.* Mort. Les
> verges et les vergers sortent de ma bouche. La sienne. Embaument ma
> poitrine si grande ouverte. Une reine-claude gonfle son silence. Silence de
> mort. Les abeilles s'echappent de ses yeux, de ses orbites où les prunelles
> ont coulé, liquides, sous les paupières flasques. Manger un adolescent
> fusillé sur les barricades, dévorer un jeune héros n'est pas chose facile.
> Nous aimons tous le soleil. J'ai la bouche en sang, et les doigts. Avec les
> dents j'ai déchiqueté la chair. Habituellement, les cadavres ne saignent pas,
> le tien si. (13–14, my emphasis)

Faced simultaneously with the murder of Jean D. and its distancing
(and/or falsification) through ideologically motivated national rituals such
as the "hommage populaire" and media coverage, the narrator reacts
viscerally. The media images of carnage thus have a paradoxical effect. On
the one hand, these images serve to create a glorified national myth—"…ce
sacrifice n'est pas perdu" says the priest, "Le petit Jean est mort pour la
France" (28)—while distancing the spectator from the death and suffering
of war, a function Genet seems to be criticizing in *Pompes funèbres*. On the
other hand, the dead, mutilated, and/or twisted body is a leitmotif of the
novel, and functions as a site of identification from which the narrator
rebuilds his memories of Jean.[21] This double movement of
distanciation/identification inherent to (violent) images is linked not only to

the qualities of the image itself, but also to death, a phenomenon referred to by Blanchot as a "cadaverous presence" which places the spectator in the realm of fascination: between here and nowhere, between reality and fiction, between the real and the fake. This is precisely the spectatorial position described by the author-narrator of *Pompes funèbres* who, in the below example, draws a comparison between the fascination produced by the sight of Jean's corpse and that of movie stars:

> Je me penchai malgré la foule afin de contempler l'enfant devenu par le miracle d'une rafale de mitrailleuse cette chose si délicate, un jeune mort. Le cadavre précieux d'un adolescent enveloppé dans les linges. Et quand la foule fut au bord du cercueil, penchée sur lui, *elle vit un visage très mince, pâle, un peu vert, le visage même de la mort sans doute, mais si banal dans sa fixité que je me demande pourquoi la Mort, les stars de cinéma, les virtuoses en voyage, les reines en exil, les rois bannis, ont un corps, un visage, des mains. Leur fascination vient d'autre chose* que d'un charme humain, et, sans tromper l'enthousiasme des paysannes qui voulaient l'apercevoir à la portière de son wagon, Sarah Bernhardt aurait pu apparaître sous la forme d'une petite boîte d'allumettes suédoises. (21, my emphasis)

The spectator, caught up in a state of fascination in the face of the image/cadaver, experiences a temporary interruption of the habitual mode in which he perceives the world. Sarah Bernhardt is a box of Swedish matches, just as, in an earlier scene, the narrator transfers Jean D.'s funeral held in honor of France into a private ceremony where the coffin, again, is a box of matches haunted by the spirits of the dead, or, as the connection with Sarah Bernhardt suggests, the magic of the image (presented here as voodoo):

> Ma boîte était sacrée. Elle ne contenait pas une parcelle du corps de Jean, elle contenait Jean tout entier. Ses ossements avaient la taille des allumettes, des cailloux emprisonnés dans les sifflets. C'était quelque chose comme ces poupées de cire enveloppées de linges, sur quoi les envoûteurs fonts leurs enchantements. (29)

The magical fascinating space created by the image, which, following Blanchot and Guillaume, allows for its ambiguities and reworkings, is posited in *Pompes funèbres* against that other, more ideologically infused use of the media that we have been discussing thus far in light of national mythology.[22] Indeed, the author-narrator, who is also simultaneously a media spectator, reveals the media to be a negotiable site of interaction and struggle through his "aberrant" readings of the media and popular culture, readings that go beyond personal or literary phantasmagoria toward a deconstruction of the very foundations of (European) identity itself (the nation representing in this text its most obvious expression).

The scene in which the narrator attends the screening of a film about the capture of members of the Vichy paramilitary militia (the "Milice") in *Pompes funèbres* is revelatory in this regard. The author-narrator, seeking to "retrouver la paix" (49), decides to go to the movies. He enters the cinema, upon which the narrative abruptly cuts to the laughter of the movie audience, a laughter provoked at the sight of a young frail *milicien* being overpowered by a French soldier:

> Tout à coup la salle éclata de rire quand le speaker dit: 'Décidément non, la guerre des toits ne nourrit pas son homme' car sur l'écran venait d'apparaître un milicien, un gamin de seize ou dix-sept ans.... Le gamin était maigre, mais beau. Son visage avait souffert. Il était triste. Il tremblait.... L'écran fut alors occupé par un bras seul armé d'une main très belle, lourde et large, puis par un jeune soldat français qui portait à l'épaule le fusil du petit traître. La salle applaudit. A nouveau revint le milicien. Son visage tremblait (les paupières surtout et les lèvres) des claques reçues à deux pas de la caméra. La salle riait, sifflait, trépignait. Le rire du monde, ni l'inélégance des caricaturistes ne m'empêcheront de reconnaître la désolante grandeur d'un milicien français qui, pendant plusieurs jours lors de l'insurrection de Paris, en août 1944, contre l'armée allemande, se retira sur les toits aux côtés des Boches, tirant jusqu'à sa dernière balle—ou l'avant-dernière—sur le peuple français qui montait les barricades. (50)

This image of the movie audience whistling, shouting insults, and laughing at the violence being done in the name of French rehabilitation establishes a continuity with the earlier media audience (the readers of the newspaper) and the crowds attending Jean D.'s funeral and homage.[23] In effect, these various groups of consumers, which constitute in sum "le peuple français," all participate in the same project: to occult the reality of the conditions brought about by the war and the occupation of France by focusing instead on those elements which favor the image of a strong French nation united in resistance not only against the Germans, but also, and perhaps even more vigorously, against French citizens who openly collaborated with the Nazi regime. Genet's presentation of these various audiences at such a crucial historical moment closely follows what Didier Anzieu has called the "group illusion" (qtd. in Robins 70). Significantly, as Robins explains, this illusion—created primarily through the screen—allows the collectivity to simultaneously expulse its fear during times of crisis and to reassert itself through a displacement of individual identity onto the group:

> The group discovers its common identity at the same time as its individual members are able to avow that they are all identical in their fears, and then that they are consensual in the defensive violence and hatred they direct against the threat that is not-us. It is a moment in which the individual can fuse with the group: for a time, at least, the defence of individual identity can be displaced onto the group. And for as long as danger and threat can be projected from its midst, the group experiences a sense of exultation through its new-found wholeness and integrity. (70)

The French media audience presented in *Pompes funèbres* clearly exhibits this "group illusion," a dynamic that is manifest in its regressive identification with the French soldier beating a so-called traitor. During times of crisis, as Anthony Giddens explains, this type of regressisve identification with a leader-figure "carries with it that essential feature of nationalism…a strong psychological affiliation with an 'in-group' coupled with a differentiation from, or rejection of, 'out-groups' (qtd. in Tomlinson 85). The young milicien being beaten on screen, and whom the narrator lovingly names Riton, incarnates the emblematic figure of the out-group and the narrator, upon witnessing his humiliation, surrenders all his love for Jean to the *image* of Riton, who henceforth figures as a central character in the novel. It is thus through Riton's image that Genet is able to sacrifice (and betray) his lover's memory in order to weave a story around his "enemies" and, in the process, to open a symbolic space for the articulation of other subjectivities that allow him to express his mourning in terms other than that of national affiliation.[24]

In effect, in *Pompes funèbres*, Genet simulates the identity of a myriad of characters, all of them connected in one way or another to his dead lover Jean D. These characters, who express different perspectives of both the war and Jean D.'s death, include Erik Seiler, a German officer who is also the lover of Jean D.'s mother; Paulo, Jean D.'s brother; Juliette, the maid of Jean D.'s mother and lover of Jean D.; and Hitler. Throughout the narrative, Genet takes up each character's identity and speaks from his or her point of view—a movement that is linked, in my view, to the inscription and centrality of media and popular culture images in the text, as well as to their importance in the broader political and social context that forms the backdrop of the novel.[25] It is as if the narrator, true to the conditions of the postmodern moment, alternates between the realm of quotidian reality (his narrative of mourning and remembrance) and the realm of the image (newspapers, cinema). This movement allows him to transform himself into a spectral subject so as to become other and, in the process, pay respect to *his* dead whom history no longer acknowledges, the dead being simply what history has passed through (Berger, *Another Way of Telling* 107). The enactment of identity in *Pompes funèbres* that is the most powerful and striking in this regard is that of the cannibal, because not only does it represent the absolute other of European identity (more "savage" even than Hitler himself) but also, and more importantly, because it holds a mirror up to the brutality of the European legacy (i.e. colonization, mass destruction, and technological rationality) through its own racialized imagery.

Earlier in this chapter, we discussed how the narrator reacts viscerally—cannibalistically—when faced with the staging of rituals guaranteed to cement national identity at the expense of Jean D.'s death. In those moments when images of heroism and patriotism in the face of carnage threaten to eclipse and pass in silence the memory and reality of Jean's death, the narrator, transforming himself into a cannibal, embraces certain "tribal" practices of devouring the dead body to appropriate its force. Speaking from within this mode, the narrator is able to assimilate the (fascist) fascination with the cult of death and turn it, through acts of voodoo, into a fascination linked not to European national identity but rather to its de-centering, a momentary disruption that deterritorializes the ideological grounding of the image (Nation) and transplants it into a (sacred) system of symbolic exchange.

The scene at the end of the novel that recounts the deaths of two primary characters, each embodying the extreme logic of nationalism, aptly illustrates this movement between national identity, individual identity, and death (non-identity). In this scene, which itself is a repetition and elaboration of both the newspaper headlines and the film scene from the beginning of the novel, we are returned to the rooftops of Paris during the Liberation, where German soldiers and French militiamen have withdrawn in order to seek shelter from the Resistance fighters. Riton, the young collaborator from the movie, and Erik Seiler, a German soldier, find themselves trapped on the rooftop with other soldiers preparing for their impending deaths. Individual identity momentarily fuses into the fascist conception of national belonging:[26]

> La cachette était étroite, elle pouvait à peine les contenir bien qu'ils se serrassent accroupis dans une sorte d'agglomération d'où la notion d'individu disparaissait. Aucune pensée ne naissait de cette masse armée, mais une somnolence, un songe dont les thèmes principaux entremêlés étaient le sentiment du vertige, la chute, la nostalgie du Vaterland. (295)

Riton and Erik disengage themselves from this "masse de mâles," and the narrator, who is also, we recall, a spectator of this film, anticipates the ensuing scenes of murder and torture by transforming himself, as Baudrillard would put it in *Symbolic Exchange and Death*, into a "primitive." Within this landscape, Paris during the days of the Liberation becomes an unnamed tropical land where members of a tribe (German soldiers and Riton shooting from the rooftops) dance around the fire in preparation for the feast to come:

> Ils roulaient la nuit sous un ciel terrible, sillonné d'éclairs de chaleur, une eau pleine d'alligators. Sur leurs bords où croissaient des fougères, les sauvages adorateurs de la lune, dans les forêts dansaient autour d'un feu. La tribu conviée au festin s'enivrait de la danse et du régal que serait ce jeune mort cuisant dans un chaudron. Il m'est doux et consolant, parmi les hommes d'un continent noir et bouleversé dont les tribus mangent leurs rois morts, de me retrouver avec les naturels de cette contrée d'Erik,

afin de pouvoir, sans danger, sans remords, manger la chair du mort le plus tendre, de pouvoir l'assimiler à la mienne, prendre avec mes doigts les meilleurs morceaux dans leur graisse, les garder sans dégoût dans ma bouche, sur ma langue, les sentir dans mon estomac et savoir que l'essentiel d'eux deviendra le meilleur de moi-même. (297)

The narrator joins in the ritual of the dance so as to loosen himself up in order to receive the sacrificial body of Jean, and, in so doing, distances himself not only from his identity as a member of the French nation, but also from the ethnicity assigned to him by the racialized politics of nation-building: "Je dansais, plus noir que les noirs au bruit du tam-tam, j'assouplissais mon corps, je le disposais à recevoir la nourriture totémique.... Assis seul à la table de bois, j'attendais que Jean, mort et nu, m'apportât lui-même, sur ses bras tendus, son propre cadavre" (297). Significantly, upon eating the "chair privilegiée," the narrator becomes a member of the tribe and, in so doing, discovers social unity within a group that is defined in opposition to the European nation-state. Death in this sense is what gives the narrator roots, a history, and it is finally from this subversive posture that he can claim to belong to France:

Seul à cette table, divinité que les nègres n'osaient fixer, je mangeai. J'appartenais à la tribu. Et non d'une façon superficielle par le seul fait de ma naissance au milieu d'elle, mais par la grâce d'une adoption où il m'était accordé de participer au festin religieux. Ainsi la mort de Jean D. m'a donné des racines. J'appartiens enfin à cette France que j'ai maudite et si fort désirée.... J'ai mes morts qui sont morts pour elle, et l'enfant abandonné a maintenant droit de cité. (298, my emphasis)

Genet's presentation of himself as a cannibal, a "primitive," in *Pompes funèbres* allows him to coopt the State's power over death, and therefore over society. As Baudrillard explains in *Symbolic Exchange and Death*, in terms which go a long way toward an understanding of Genet's preoccupation with criminals, murder, and violence and their entanglement with works of art and images,

every death and all violence that escapes the State monopoly is subversive; it is a prefiguration of the abolition of power. Hence the fascination wielded by great murderers, bandits or outlaws, which is in fact closely akin to that associated with works of art: a piece of death and violence is snatched from the State monopoly in order to be put back into the savage, direct and symbolic reciprocity of death, just as something in feasting and expenditure is retrieved from the economic in order to be put back into useless and sacrificial exchange, and just as something in the poem or the artwork is retrieved from the terrorist economy of signification in order to be put back into the consumption of signs. This alone is what is fascinating in our system.... Millions of war dead are exchanged as values in accordance with a general equivalence: 'dying for the fatherland;'.... Only certain deaths, certain practices, escape this convertibility; they alone are subversive, but do not often make the headlines. (175)

By representing nationalist efforts to appropriate the war dead through the eyes of media spectators, especially the movie audience, Genet places emphasis not only on the factitious nature of national identity itself,[28] but also on culture's fascination with the spectacle of death and its conversion to State power.[28] But the dead in *Pompes funèbres* inevitably win out over the State. Indeed, the final media images of this text testify to death's subversive force over society, and suggest, at the same time, its potential to reunite people through its binding and irrevocable ties:

Les Japonais, rapportent les journaux, one conseillé à leurs soldats de lutter même après la mort, que leurs âmes soutiennent et dirigent les vivants.... La beauté d'une telle objurgation (qui me montre un ciel débordant d'une activité en puissance, plein de morts s'efforçant de tirer) m'incite à faire prononcer par Riton cette phrase: —Aide-moi à mourir. (307)

Media Images Incarnated: The Living-Dead of *Les Paravents*

The image that appears at the end of *Pompes funèbres* of soldiers combating well after their deaths, supporting and guiding the living, becomes a "reality," albeit a theatrical one, in *Les Paravents*. Indeed, this play, which also takes its inspiration from current events, starts and finishes in the realm of the dead: death frames the entire play from the outset via the image (the play is dedicated "à la mémoire d'un jeune mort") and most of the characters burst through screens during the play to pass from life to death. The passing from life to death is, however, not a linear projectory but rather a circular one. As Odette Aslan explains, "[p]artie d'une anecdote réelle" (le maçon algérien qui s'était fait voler ses économies et ne pouvait plus s'acheter qu'une femme laide), la pièce 'ne célèbre rien' mais se veut une fête donnée à l'intention des Morts" (14). *Les Paravents* is thus designed, as Genet writes to Roger Blin, "to illuminate the world of the dead" (*Reflections* 11) and to create at the same time, as in *Pompes funèbres*, a space for symbolic exchange with them. In effect, this play could be seen as a gesture created specifically for the dead in the space *par excellence* of death: the theatre.[29] As Genet writes,

> I say this to you because the spectacle, so limited in time and space, seemingly intended for a handful of spectators, will be so serious that it will also be aimed at the dead. No one must be turned away from or deprived of the spectacle: it must be so beautiful that the dead are made beautiful too, and blush because of it. If you stage *The Screens*, you must always work with the notion of a unique spectacle in mind, and carry it as far as you can. *Everything should work together to break down whatever separates us from the dead.* We must do everything possible towards creating the feeling that we have worked for them, and that we have succeeded. (*Reflections* 12, my emphasis)

Genet's ideas about the stage as a site "closely akin to death" echo those of Anne Ubersfeld presented in her "Kantor ou La Parole de la Mort" in which she discusses *le théâtre de la mort*. "Le théâtre est fait avec la mort," she writes, "il ne se conçoit pas sans elle, il donne à voir des personnages hors leur existence quotidienne…. Mais le moindre personnage quotidien qui évolue sur une scène est marqué par la possibilité qui est la sienne de mourir ou d'être déjà mort. Pourtant la mort théâtrale est faite d'irréalité, niée par la présence physique, vivante du comédien" (251).

How is one to stage death, asks Ubersfeld, without recourse to rudimentary artifice (*artifice grossier*)? Kantor's answer is strikingly similar to Genet's insofar as, according to Ubersfeld, "[Kantor] jou[e] sur une figure de rhétorique capitale au théâtre, mais à laquelle il fait rendre tout ce qu'elle peut donner. Je veux parler de l'*oxymore* : il ne faut pas montrer les morts comme morts, mais comme morts-vivants, ou mieux, comme vivants-morts, comme vivants toujours-déjà morts, chargés de figurer des morts vivant quelque part" (251). Media images, precisely because they place the spectator into a realm of fascination that figures the world of the dead through their "cadaverous presence," are, for Genet, a privileged vehicle in the creation of the oxymoronic space of the living-dead referred to here by Ubersfeld.

The macabre denseness of the imagery of "national imagining" and its cult of death present in *Pompes funèbres*, however, becomes more playful and plastic in *Les Paravents* due, in large part, to the artifice of theater. Nevertheless, despite the shift in tone and register, this play, written in 1958 and edited in 1961, addresses many of the same mechanisms at work throughout the novel. In what follows, I will again take up Genet's vision of history as simulation to focus on the mediatrix at work in the construction and deployment of the imperial imaginary and identity. I will then consider the ways in which Genet inscribes culturally coded (media) images as a means for creating a space of intercultural connection, a space which ultimately culminates in death.

Imperialism, Nationalism, and Interculturality in Technicolor

Les Paravents stands out in French literary history as the only substantial work to be written on the Algerian War by a French playwright during the time that the war was taking place.[30] Sharing with *Les Nègres* a concern for staging the colonial apparatus (replete with its racial and sexual images, distortions, and power plays) from the point of view of both the colonizers and the colonized, *Les Paravents* also recalls the theatricalization of power in modern society which is so convincingly portrayed in *Les Bonnes* (1947), *Haute surveillance* (1949), and *Le Balcon* (1956).[31]

What differentiates *Les Paravents* from Genet's other theatrical pieces, however, is the fact that unlike his other plays in which the power structure is staged in remote and rather unlikely circumstances (that is, the make-believe), *Les Paravents*, although equally artificial in its techniques, strikes at the very heart of French society at a time when, similar to *Pompes funèbres*, the (implied) context of the play could not be ignored or distanced. The reasons for this are many. In the 1960s, not only was there an enormous silence in France surrounding the decolonization of Algeria, but French society was in the process of reabsorbing around a million *piedsnoirs*. Moreover, as David Bradby points to, at this time General de Gaulle's "declared aim was to move France into a position where it could turn its back on its colonial past, and start to play a major role in the new technological revolution that was transforming the industrialized countries of the world" (1). It is thus not surprising that upon the staging of *Les Paravents* in Paris by Roger Blin in 1966, fighting broke out both in the theater and on the streets. Most certainly, this had everything to do with Genet's portrayal of French soldiers as nothing more than seductive, vapid images of power, carefully groomed and maintained so as to reflect the image of France itself (just as, in *Pompes funèbres*, the German soldiers mirrored the Fürher and, by analogy, Germany itself):

> **LE LIEUTENANT**: ...Que chaque homme pour n'importe quel autre soit un miroir. Deux jambes doivent se regarder et se voir dans les deux jambes d'en face, un torse dans le torse d'en face, la bouche dans une autre bouche, les yeux dans les yeux, le nez dans le nez, les dents dans les dents, les genoux dans les genoux, une boucle de cheveux dans...une autre ou si les cheveux d'en face sont raides dans un accroche-coeur... (*Très lyrique.*) S'y regarder et s'y voir d'une parfaite beauté... (*Il fait un demi-tour réglementaire et parle face au public.*) d'une totale séduction. Et que se multiplient encore les miroirs à trois faces, à dix faces, à treize, à cent treize, à mille, à cent mille! Que les profils se renvoient des profils et que l'image que vous offrirez aux rebelles soit d'une si grande beauté, que leur image qu'ils ont d'eux ne pourra pas résister. Vaincue. Elle tombera en morceaux. Cassée.... Ou comme la glace: fondue. Victoire sur l'ennemi: morale. (182)

The seductive power (or, in Genet's terms, the "phénomène de grossissement") of the mechanically reproduced image and its importance in the maintenance of the imperial imagination is symbolized here by the serialized reflection of a beautiful French soldier. This (homoerotic) image of soldiers intertwined one within the other and mirroring each other to perfection brings to mind colonial adventure stories which, as Joseph Bristow explains, provided European and American men a space in which to become "aggrandized subjects" (qtd. in Shohat and Stam 101). Perhaps more importantly, however, the serialized image of a beautiful soldier conjures up a complete register of media technologies such as newspapers, advertisements, and film that had, since the early twentieth century, fostered a national self-consciousness which supported the imperial project of empire.

Indeed, alongside the image of the beautiful soldier, media technologies also presented images of the orient, its colors and costumes, which have long constituted an object of fascination for what Shohat and Stam refer to as the "imperial imaginary." From the appeal of the *bayadère* and the *odalisque* in cabaret dances, paintings and photographs in *fin de siècle* France to the covers of American tourist and fashion magazines today, the *mise en image* of the orient through its colors, fabrics, and clothing has served—in opposition to the austere, colorless costumes of Western (male) clothing—as a trope in the creation of a "feminized" and fantastic orient that allows the imagination to "go native," crossing over as it were into "a world of romance without boundaries" (Shohat and Stam 168).

Ostensibly drawing from this long tradition of orientalist representation, Genet, in *Un Captif amoureux* (1986), similarly evokes alluring colors and fabrics in what would seem to be a description of Palestinian camps as seen by the narrator from afar. The myriad of colors and fabrics here operates, in accordance with colonialist and ethnographic modes of representation, to construct an exotic orient, an inviting, mysterious place of peace and harmony, joy and happiness or, to put it bluntly, a great place to take a holiday. In the following example, the mythologizing dimensions of orientalist representation are underlined by the presence of both fog and the veil, which itself is a standard metonymical device frequently called upon to obfuscate the diversity of the *Machrek* and the *Maghreb*. Genet writes,

> Que les voiles soient de mille couleurs obtenues par des pièces de tissu afin de boucher une déchirure, cela plaisait à l'oeil, à l'occidental surtout. En voyant, d'assez loin et un jour de brume, les camps, on les supposait emplis de bonheur tellement chaque pièce de toile coloriée semblait choisie pour aller avec la couleur des autres, et cette harmonie ne pouvait recouvrir qu'un peuple joyeux puisqu'il avait su faire de son camp la joie des yeux. (22)

A few ligns later we realize that, in fact, this description is based not on the narrator's eye-witness testimony, but rather on representations of the orient taken from "les revues de luxe" provided to airline passengers in which "le papier glacé donne aux campements une apparence de grande paix" (22). The aesthetic spectacle offered by the harmonious colors is thus, for the Westerner, a comforting *trompe-l'oeil*: much like the topos of the veil, the colors and fabrics of the photographed Palestinian camps cover and conceal, through their transformation into exotic objects of consumption, the fact that these camps, far from existing in a state close to paradise as suggested by the travel ad, are, in Genet's words, "les détritus de nations 'assises'" (22). By turning orientalism itself into an object of representation, Genet underscores its artificial, mediated dimension as well as its political consequences. Indeed, in terms which poetically reverse the effect of the *trompe-l'oeil*, he advises us to look beyond the sheen of appearance:

> Nous devions nous défendre contre cette élégance qui eût pu nous faire croire que le bonheur était là, sous tant de fantaisie, tout de même qu'il faut regarder avec défiance les photos de camps au soleil sur le papier glacé des magazines de luxe. Un coup de vent fit tout voler, voiles, toiles, zinc, tôle, et je vis au jour le malheur. (22)

The simulacral media images of Palestinian life in this sense continue the pictorial tradition of empire present in cinema, painting, and photographs at the turn of the century, even while they displace it into a postmodern or global context: Imperialism in *Un Captif amoureux* shifts away from the strictly colonial paradigm toward the much more contradictory and diffuse paradigm of Eurocentrism and globalization.[32] In his critique of the media, Genet denounces the cultural hegemony reflected in the glossy pages of expensive magazines—where Palestinians do not, for the most part, represent themselves but rather are always re-presented— even while he creates a space for intercultural interaction through the use of a "we" subject which implies readers well aware of the pitfalls of cultural representation.

The space of interculturality as a space of conflicting images is also evident in *Les Paravents*. In this play, as later in *Un Captif amoureux*, the question of cultural otherness, as well as the power of one culture to impose itself on another, is raised primarily as a politics of *image*. As the French Lieutenant remarks to the Sergeant after the onset of war with the Arabs, "Ce n'est pas d'intelligence qu'il s'agit: mais de perpétuer une image qui a plus de dix siècles, qui va se fortifiant à mesure que ce qu'elle doit figurer s'effrite" (181). Indeed, in *Les Paravents*, Genet presents history as little more than a process of image making performed primarily in the service of capitalist modernity and the nation-state, or what is commonly referred to in critical discourse as Western cultural imperialism. History in Genet's hands asserts itself, in line with media culture, as a simulacrum which, nevertheless, produces reality effects due to its ability to shape individual and collective identities and subjectivities by means of the spaces it creates for cultural belonging. National, cultural or ethnic identities are only a few byproducts of this process. As Monsieur Blankensee, a colonist who pads his clothing with cushions to create the aura of a powerful silhouette maintains, history as the artificial container of falsely constructed identities is necessary "Pour l'équilibre. Un homme de mon âge qui n'a ni ventre ni cul n'a guère de prestige. Alors, il faut bien truquer un peu.... Autrefois, il y avait les perruques.... Oui, il faut tout ce trucage pour nous imposer...pour en imposer!" (113). In other words, the virility which is so carefully constructed by the colonists and the military in the form of dress and accoutrements (including fake shoulders, buttocks and various other body parts) reflects an imbalance at the core of the patriarchal capitalist culture itself. As Judith Williamson remarks, "Capitalism is not a system which can function alone in equilibrium. It always needs some imbalance, something other than itself: riddled with contradictions, it is not internally sufficient" (112).

In the theatrical context of *Les Paravents*, as the above example demonstrates, one way Genet stages these imbalances is through the presentation of colonial history as a process of simulation and the production of false (national) identities. He accomplishes this for the most part via an elaborate use of theatrical objects such as clothing, color, and make-up, themselves drawn not from "reality" but rather from popularized image culture. Indeed, not unlike orientalist technicolor productions such as travel posters, film, photographs, museum exhibits, and television programs which make use of color and costume to exoticize and "feminize" the orient, so does Genet rely on a process of technicolor, in conjunction with costuming devices, to forge images of national stereotypes. In this sense, the screens of the title of the play define, as Laura Oswald remarks, "the physical surfaces of film or television" ("Middle East Voices" 49). They also demonstrate the mass-mediated style of national imagining, not to mention cultural identities themselves.

In *Les Paravents*, vestimentary codes and performative devices implement on one level a hierarchical structure that differentiates the colonizers from the colonized. At the same time, however, clichéd dress functions as a signifier of outrageous theatricality. For example, the cultural imagining of nationality for the French is presented throughout the play as a sharp, clearly focused, larger than life image which is reflected by their impeccable clothing and tricolored make-up. "Le Légionnaire," specifies Genet in his commentary on the second tableau, "comme tous les soldats et tous les Européens, sera très grand, monté sur des semelles et des talons de vingt ou trente centimètres. Epaules très larges. Uniforme très ajusté et très soigné. Képi perché sur l'oeil. Maquillage du visage: bleu, blanc, rouge" (37). Literally and figuratively "dressed to kill," backed by a centuries-old image of a glorious national past, the victory of the French over the Arabs is, in the mouth of the Lieutenant, virtually a sure thing:

> La France a déjà vaincu, c'est-à-dire qu'elle a proposé une image ineffaçable. Donc, pas vaincre, mais mourir. Ou mourir à demi, c'est-à-dire rentrer éclopés, pattes en moins, reins perdus, couilles arrachées, nez mangés, faces rôties…c'est aussi très bien…. Ainsi dans l'image de ses guerriers qui pourissent, la France pourra se regarder pourrir… (180)

It is important to note here that *la pourriture* is overcoded as a positive attribute in *Les Paravents*, signifying as it does the achievement of an image of perfection, or, in other words, death. Martyred soldiers in a nationalistic context serve only to strengthen patriotic ties, and guarantee if not a military victory, then at least a moral one. As one of the European figures, the Banker, suggests, this type of victory, won on the field of representation, may be even more significant. Facing the impending defeat of the French army, the Banker declares,

Et nous, nous avons au moins la possibilité de nous retrancher derrière notre noblesse ancestrale et derrière notre noblesse morale. Tout est gagné et depuis longtemps. Eux qu'ont-ils donc? Ils n'ont rien. Surtout ne leur accordez jamais la possibilité d'être des héros: ils oseraient s'en prévaloir. (250)

In the face of this solidified and unshakeable image of the French nation, which is staged, as we have been discussing, primarily through clichéd dress popularized by mass media images, the Arabs, on the other hand, are clothed, true to orientalist patterns, in technicolored costumes many of which are composed (like the Palestinian camps) of bits and pieces of fabric in varying shades of the same color. The Mother's dress, as Genet details in his *Letters to Roger Blin*, "is made of rags from various cloths, of a variety of forms and materials, in different shades of purple and mauve. The seams will be visible, the rags having been pieced together with a course white thread" (*Reflections* 27). Similarly, the dress of Kadidja, another powerful matriarch in the play, "will be yellow. Every possible yellow, a patchwork of saffron, ochre, etc." In addition, the make-up of the Arab characters is to be multicolored, such that, as Genet writes to Roger Blin, "it must remind one of, must call to mind, Algeria by methods of which the Algerians are unaware.... Algerian poverty and misery must have other colours and other materials, which must be discovered" (15).

In contradistinction to the clean and sober, albeit grotesque, appearance of the European figures, therefore, the Arabs wear a mask of dust, filth, and disease composed by macabre make-up which externalizes and renders visible the racist association of whiteness to cleanliness and its corollary, darkness to dirtiness. Saïd, to take but one example, has "le creux des joues très noir, et autour, des pustules jaunâtres—ou verdâtres." In addition, "C'est un malpropre. Et je ne parle pas de sa puanteur. On n'a plus de force quand il est à deux pas. Toute l'équipe est contaminée, déshonorée!..." reports a fellow Arab worker to the colonist Sir Harold in an attempt to distance himself from Saïd who is a reported thief (Tableau X 109). To which Sir Harold retorts, "Alors, qu'il vous vole ou non, qu'il vous plaise ou déplaise, c'est un Arabe comme les autres" (109). The dominance of the Europeans, as well as the reduction of various Arab characters to the quintessential Arab, are further underscored by a final sartorial manoeuvre—whereas the European figures are all mounted on platform shoes and high heels, the Arabs are "pieds nus" with "le dos voûté," thus indicating their servile and lowly status.

All of these elements combined reflect not only the distorted and inverted picture of the colonized as they are portrayed in orientalist and Eurocentric discourses. They also demonstrate the extent to which identity, for Genet, has no foundation—unless, of course, we are talking about make-up. Rather, for Genet, identity—whether it be national, cultural, sexual, or ethnic—is purely a matter of image. In this context, the comments made by the Général to the Lieutenant make perfect sense:

> **LE GENERAL**: Je me le demande, après vingt-huit ans de service, si je n'avais pas admiré ma prestance dans une glace, est-ce que j'aurais eu assez de courage pour la défendre?.... Si jamais, en face, il leur tombe un miroir entre les pattes.

> **LE LIEUTENANT**: J'ai donné l'ordre qu'on tire d'abord sur les glaces. (188)

Costume and color in *Les Paravents* are thus used not as authentic or essentialized concepts of French or Arab/Algerian identity. Rather they are, as Helen Gilbert remarks in another context, "a recognition, through self-conscious parody, of the ways in which [these groups] have been looked at in the discourses of theater, film, and especially tourism" (127). Tableau XII of *Les Paravents*, in which a group of French colonists/tourists is assembled to "observe" the indigenous culture, exemplifies the gaze of the Eurocentric media spectator even while it parodies it. Indeed, the characters gathered in this tableau, which include an academic, a soldier, a vamp, a journalist, a judge, a banker, and "une petite communiante" (145), could even be seen as a representative sample of the French population, similar to the mechanisms of statistical surveys today. The following dialogue between the vamp, the academic, the soldier, and the journalist demonstrates the extent to which the cultural/imperial imaginary of the French vis-à-vis the Arabs is mediated by a vision informed, for the most part, by (touristic) images:

LA VAMP, *riant*: Mais où sont vos sauvages? De cette révolte ne voit pas grand-chose? Les soulèvements...
LE SOLDAT: Dans mon caleçon, mademoiselle...
L'ACADEMICIEN, *l'interrompant*: Romains. Sans vous pas de routes. Et si pas de routes pas de facteurs. Et si pas de facteurs pas de cartes postales. (*Un temps.*) Et ils continuent à prendre les chemins de traverse...
LE REPORTER-PHOTOGRAPHE: Sen-sa-tion-nel! Un cliché sensationnel! Les fameuses mouches d'Orient, énormes, bouleversantes. Autour du cadavre et jusqu'au coin des yeux des gamins. La photo bourdonnait! (145–47)

This play's emphasis on theatricality, highlighted in the above example by the artifice of photography, thus allows "for the effective subversion of imperial authority through the visual excesses of the carnivalesque, here mobilized primarily in opposition to the...multiple oppressions" of the colonial system (Gilbert 127).

If Genet inscribes stereotypical costume and color as a primary means to distinguish between the colonizers and the colonized, these elements nevertheless are also used to create a space of intercultural connection through their ability to provoke audiences to shift their perspective, that is, to see themselves clothed as the "other of their others" (Gilbert 124). We recall here that while clothing is used to differentiate the French and the Europeans from the Arabs in *Les Paravents*, both groups are played by the same actors. As we read in the didascalia, "Chaque acteur sera tenu de jouer le rôle de cinq ou six personnages, hommes ou femmes" (15). "This doubling technique," to borrow again from Gilbert's post-colonial reading of costume in Australian theatre, "sets up an immediate paradox: despite the differences signified by their clothes, once two characters are introduced by the same actor, each carries the traces of the other throughout the action, a process which thwarts the formation of an unproblematically delineated character" (121).

While foregrounded initially as divisive markers, then, clothing and color in *Les Paravents*, like the image culture that popularized them, are also sites of intercultural struggle. For instance, in the first tableau of the play we are introduced to two Arab characters, the Mother and Saïd, who are on their way to Saïd's wedding. When they stop momentarily to rest, the

Mother, appropriating the colors of France in the form of high heel shoes one of which is white and the other red (she, we recall, is wearing a violet dress), performs a dance that at once parodies French female historical emblems such as Joan of Arc or Marianne, and annonces the Mother as emblem of the Arab revolution to come. As Saïd declares, "Sur vos pattes incassables, la vieille, dansez! Et vous aussi, cailloux, regardez donc ce qui se passe au-dessus de vous. Que ma vieille vous piétine comme une révolution le pavé des rois...Hourrah!...Boum! Boum! (*Il imite le canon*)" (23).

  This carnivalesque play with cultural imagery is not limited to a strictly nationalistic context. In effect, throughout *Les Paravents*, performance and masquerade introduce disjunctive elements between the actor and his or her clothing, "preventing the seamless application of clothing to the performer/character, [and] suggesting that its race and gender connotations are highly arbitrary" (Gilbert 107). The shifting identity of the Gendarme as he crosses from male to female dress aptly illustrates this premise. Speaking to two muslim women, the Gendarme declares,

> Les musulmanes! Si je les connais, vos astuces!.... Un jour de carnaval, avec un drap et un torchon, je m'étais déguisé en moukère, en fatma; d'un coup, d'un seul j'ai compris votre mentalité. Tout dans l'oeil. Et si les circonstances m'y obligent, malgré ma blessure et mes deux filles, je reprends le voile. (*Dans la couverture il s'enroule ainsi qu'il le dit et il quitte la scène*) (103)

  The gender displacement undergone by the speaking subject in this passage (itself coded as a carnivalesque subversion of cultural power) demonstrates the creative potential of cross-cultural contact (as clothing changes, so does perspective) and indicates that mixed-dress codes may operate, in some cases, as a form of cultural negotiation even while they announce acculturation in others. *Les Paravents* is quite specific in its construction of clothing as a colonizing tool. However, carnivalesque disruptions of sartorial power inevitably code the play as a burlesque circus in which clothing takes on a life of its own. Sir Harold's glove, which is capable of watching over his Arab workers while he is away, provides a particularly humorous example. The scene occurs in Tableau IV. In response to Habib's question, "Vous partez déjà Sir Harold?", Sir Harold responds: "'Pas tout à fait. Mon gant vous gardera.' Un merveilleux gant de pécari arrive, jeté de la coulisse. Il reste comme suspendu dans l'air, au milieu de la scène" (51). By separating clothing—the *image* of colonial power—from its locus of power, that is the physical presence of the colonizer, Genet is able to reveal the multiple relays of power at work within the paradigm of cultural imperialism, and expose, at the same time, its vested interests.

Media Imperialism: The "Bleaching-out" of Death?

Thus far, we have examined the ways in which Genet uses the images projected from national and historical landscapes in order to parody the values for which they stand. At the same time, however, the space of the screen in *Les Paravents* is also a space of intercultural exchange and ultimately this space, while carrying the potential for cultural homologization, belongs, as in *Pompes funèbres*, to the dead. Tableau VI, in which the village women go to cry for the dead (an activity they have excluded Saïd's mother from due to her family's position as outcasts), demonstrates the extent to which the globalization of cultural imagery (especially images that rob culture of its dead) represents a threat to traditional, if not sacred, customs of respecting the dead.

In this scene, Genet introduces a brand-name commercial item—"la Javel Lacroix"—into a conversation between three Arab women on their way to visit a marabout's graveside. This advertisement highlights European racialized imagery and its association of the Other with death—a form of social exclusion, as Baudrillard reminds us in *Symbolic Exchange and Death*, that accompanied the trajectory of reason in modernity. Perhaps more importantly, however, it also demonstrates the increasing marginalization of death and the dead from the modern landscape, especially in the face of the globalization of Western media:

CHIGHA, *environ quarante ans. Elle marche à petits pas venant de droite, vers la coulisse de gauche. Elle crie.* Dépêchez-vous. Si on est en retard, il n'y aura plus de mouches! (Fredonnant.) Les mouches! Les mouches! Les mouches!...

KADIDJA, *environ soixante ans*: Même en hiver quelqu'un a connu un mort sans mouches? Cadavre sans mouches, sinistre cadavre. Elles font partie, les mouches, du deuil...

CHIGHA, *riant*: Alors, ma maison est en deuil depuis longtemps. On y enterre à longueur de journée, probablement: elle est portée par les mouches. Mouches dans les caves, mouches au plafond, et leurs merdes sur ma peau...

NEDJMA, *vingt ans, avec un visible dégoût*: Si les étrangers nous méprisent, c'est parce qu'il y a encore des femmes comme toi. Ils ont inventé la Javel Lacroix pour nous décrasser. Leurs femmes restent... (64)

It is not surprising that the reproach made to the women here comes from a woman of the younger generation since for her, culture is defined primarily by what she sees on television and buys in the supermarket. On one level, this fictional reference to a commercial image recalls Balandier's comment that in today's societies, younger generations acquire cultural knowledge primarily through commercials, television or filmic images, and rock music instead of through literature or political ideologies (15). On another level, however, Nedjma's remarks concerning "la Javel Lacroix" reflect a larger cultural transformation relative to a shift in the colonial paradigm—where once cultural imperialism was enacted through holy wars in the name of religious ideology (symbolized in the image of Lacroix), now it is conceived as the product of "media imperialism" brought about by the spread of Western cultural norms through the global diffusion of Western products and their underlying ideology. In line with the Baudrillardian model of simulation, Western images here take on the allure of contagious bacteria sent to infiltrate and alter, via a "bleaching" process, the memories of those who have historically been oppressed by the very ideology to which they now subscribe. Nedjma lives in fact not in the Algeria represented by a harsh sun, dust, flies and the hammam, but rather in the domain of the hyperreal:

CHIGHA: ...dix heures dans l'eau chaude. Dix heures à cuire au bain-marie. Moi aussi, je vais au hammam...pour promener après mes deux arpions blancs dans la poussière...

NEDJMA, *ramassant le parapluie pour se protéger du soleil*: Moi, plus tard, je vivrai à l'italienne. Dans ma chambre, ni mouches ni cafards... (64)

However, if Nedjma has been sucessfully seduced by the image of a clean European way of life, it is due perhaps less to Western "media imperialism" than to the fact that within this consumer fantasy, the face of death has vanished (significantly, in Nedjma's room *à l'italienne*, there are no more flies or roaches, two symbols par excellence of death). It is clear that cultural goods, including the media, cannot be seen as having a unilateral cultural effect. John Tomlinson reiterates this point in his book *Cultural Imperialism* (1991) when he remarks that "People in modern societies may watch a lot of television, but they do many other things besides, and to overemphasize the representational aspects of cultural action and experience is, perhaps, to end up with a rather narrow view of culture" (23). This view is supported in *Les Paravents* by the fact that although Nedjma's desires have been "contaminated" by the Western image of a society without dirt and insects, and thus without death, the desires of two other characters in the play, Saïd and Leïla, have not—in fact, although these three Arab youths belong to the same cultural milieu, their desires are radically opposite. Where Nedjma seeks a safe-haven away from the dirty realities of everyday life (a desire that could be read as her internalization of European bourgeois socio-cultural norms), Saïd and Leïla seek to plunge themselves deeper and deeper into mire and filth until they reach a state of ultimate abjection:

> **SAID**, *continuant une conversation avec Leïla*: Dans ma cellule aussi il fait noir. La seule lumière c'est tes dents gâtées, tes yeux sales, ta peau triste, qui me l'apportent. Tes yeux fameux, tes yeux fumeux, l'un qui vise Rio de Janeiro et l'autre qui plonge dans le fond d'une tasse: ça c'est toi. Et ta peau triste: un vieux cache-col en soie autour du cou d'un instituteur laïque: ça, c'est toi. Mes yeux n'arrivent plus à s'en détacher...
> **LEILA**: Moi aussi j'ai mis de la bonne volonté à descendre où tu me disais et c'est pas au fond d'une tasse de lait! Maintenant, j'y vais toute seule. Et même, il faudrait presque me retenir par la jupe... (128–9)

The appropriation of this abjection closely associated with death throughout *Les Paravents* is perhaps best exemplified by Warda, the quintessential prostitute. Warda is indeed not an ordinary prostitute, nor is she part of everyday life. In fact, when we meet her, she is already dead, that is a simulacrum of the Ideal prostitute. In the didascalia, Warda (whose name in Arabic means Rose) appears to us wearing a "robe de tissu d'or, très lourd, mêmes souliers, mais rouges, cheveux en un énorme chignon, rouge sang, visage très pale" (27). And while it might first appear that Warda is but a tried and true cliché of a long line of literary prostitutes (notably those that people the novels of Balzac and the poetry of Gautier, Baudelaire and Mallarmé), she nevertheless is different because *she knows that she is dead*, that is, nothing more than an allegory, a sacred image, a simulacrum. It is for this reason that Warda appears to us self-consciously (parodically) as a statue, a tomb, ancient ruins (thus conjuring up the lexicon of death and sexuality). Her identity exists only through ritual (simulation), that is as her clothing, her make-up and her style:

> **WARDA**, *à la Servante, d'une voix traînante*. Epais...plus épais le blanc sur mes chevilles. (*Elle se cure les dents avec une longue épingle à chapeau à tête dorée.*) ...C'est le blanc qui tient la peau tendue... (*Elle crache au loin ce qu'elle avait entre les dents.*) Complètement gâtée...Tout le fond de ma bouche est en ruine. (28)

> **WARDA**, *comptant ses bracelets*. Il en manque un, tu l'apporteras. Je dois être lourde. (*Un silence, et, comme pour elle-même.*) Manque un bracelet! Comme si j'étais un cercueil et qu'il manque un coup de marteau. (*A Mustapha:*) La nuit commence par l'habillage, la peinture. Quand le soleil est tombé je ne pourrais rien faire sans mes parures...même écarter les jambes pour pisser je ne pourrais, mais juponnée d'or, je suis la Reine des Averses. (28)

Warda, because she is nothing more than a simulacrum, appears to us as a spectral image. Beneath her clothing and make-up, she is nothing more than "une squelette soutenant des robes dorées" (199). Moreover, it is via her movement from in front of the screen to behind the screen that she performs as a prostitute:

> **WARDA**, parlant en direction de la scène, où il n'y a personne, et repoussant Mustapha qui s'approchait: Déboutonne-toi, Saïd, je monte. (A la Servante:) La cuvette?
> **LA SERVANTE**: Rincée. Warda passe derrière le paravent, très solennelle. Un assez long silence. (35)

In fact, in Tableau XIV, it is only when "reality" interferes with Warda's existence as a simulacrum—that is when the Algerian war invades the whorehouse in the form of angry soldiers who appropriate death for the value of the State—that Warda feels she is becoming only Warda, an ordinary prostitute with a singular meaning, and therefore a living person: "Moi, Warda, les hommes venaient de loin pour me voir me curer les dents avec mes grandes épingles à chapeau. Maintenant, ils viennent pour me baiser" (198). The more the "real" world enters into the whorehouse, desecrating it as one would a cadaver or a tomb, the less the whorehouse is associated with another world or the realm of the dead. As Warda remarks, "Le bordel n'est plus le bordel et pour ainsi dire, on baise à ciel ouvert. Notre travail est devenu aussi clair que celui des femmes au lavoir. La nuit? …elle est partie. La nuit qui nous entourait, qui l'a soufflée" (199)? At this precise moment, the moment when reality and fiction are no longer distinct one from the other and death has been definitively chased from the scene, Warda finds a certain identity, that of the (consumer-oriented) prostitute: "Pute! Moi, Warda," she declares, "qui devais de plus en plus m'effacer pour ne laisser à ma place qu'une pute parfaite, simple squelette soutenant des robes dorées et me voici à fond de train redevenir Warda" (199).

Warda's trajectory from death to life, or from spectrality to a fixed identity, marks the progressive stages of the elimination of the dead from the realm of the living and the subsequent loss of symbolic exchange with death. In other words, the more Warda (or death) is appropriated by/for the living (Warda compares the whorehouse to a factory), the more her alterity fades and eventually becomes non-existant (she becomes a mere product of consumption). In Les Paravents, every character traces this movement save for two, Saïd and his wife Leïla. It is my contention that their irrecuperable nature has much less to do with their dedication to le Mal as critics have argued. Rather, in their refusal to surrender their deaths to the cause of war and patriotic nationalism (whether on the part of the French or the Arabs), their gesture can be read as the ultimate resistence to consumer culture. They indeed are the only elements that maintain a symbolic exchange with death.

Philip Watts has observed that "[a]s a character in his own work, Genet is constantly confronted with media images and is decidedly writing against them" (191). What I hope to have demonstrated in this chapter is that Genet, while recognizing and criticizing the use of images to support national, historical, and empirical forms of rationalism, nevertheless restores the image, against the grain of reason, to "the sensuous, the particular, and the ephemeral" (Berger, *Another Way* 122). He does this by placing the image at the center of subjective processes where it operates, in lieu of an originary subject, to create constantly evolving identities grounded in personal, often visceral experience. As Genet's dismantling not just of French identity, but of the very notion of identity itself in *Pompes funèbres* and *Les Paravents* has underlined, images can help us to see that "the self is fractured because our social experience requires it of us—more from some than others; the experience of 'unity' of identity is nothing more than the privilege of being at home in the dominant culture, of feeling integrated within it" (Bordo, *Twilight Zones* 212). At the same time, images can potentially help us to rediscover the world in playful, adaptable, nonimperialist modes. In Genet's case, this opening onto the world begins and ends in our reunion with death and with our ghosts, both future and past.

NOTES

1. See Laura Oswald's study *Jean Genet and the Semiotics of Performance* (1989); Gene A. Plunka's *The Rites of Passage of Jean Genet* (1992); and Scott Durham's dissertation *The Poetics of Simulation: The Simulacrum and Narrative in the Works of Jean Genet and Pierre Klossowski* (1992) to name only a few more recent examples.

2. As comments from an obituary in the *National Review* demonstrate: "Jean Genet, RIP NOVELIST, playwright, prose master, and Parisian cult anti-hero, Jean Genet was a striking figure in that he cared enough about Western culture to attack it in every conceivable detail. Nothing important went un-negated.... All of the West's virtues he depicted as vices; all of its vices became for him virtues" (1).

3. Laura Oswald devotes a substantial part of her work on Genet to demonstrating this premise. In "Middle East Voices," she writes: "Throughout his work Genet criticizes the claim of classical mimesis to hold a mirror to transcendent reality and to deliver the truth in the guise of a perfect copy. He exposes the elaborate ideological and technological apparatus at work in classical mimesis which ensures the infinite reinscription of the values, claims, and identity of the dominant, European culture in representations of history.... He opens discourse to the possibility of multiple subject positions and points of view and provides means of accounting for the unrepresentable difference separating the dominant culture from its racial, sexual, and social others" (52).

4. It is important to note that throughout his work, Genet insists on the fact that works of art, especially his own, are not direct forms of social or political transformation. In his view, "Ce qu'on appelle révolutions poétiques ou artistiques ne sont pas exactement des révolutions. Je ne crois pas qu'elles changent l'ordre du monde. Elles ne changent pas non plus la vision qu'on a du monde. Elles affinent la vision, elles la complètent, elles la rendent plus complexe, mais elles ne la transforment pas du tout au tout, comme une révolution sociale ou politique" (*Dialogues* 20).

5. In *Postmodernist Fiction*, Brian McHale addresses the use of media technologies in fiction writing toward the creation of a heterotopian space: "As the novel unfolds," he writes, "our world and the 'other world' mingle with increasing intimacy, hallucinations and fantasies become real, metaphors become literal, the fictional worlds of mass media—the movies, comic-books—thrust

themselves into the midst of historical reality" (45). We will return to this dynamic further in the course of our discussion.

6. The globalization of Western media technologies cannot be conflated with the larger problematic of cultural imperialism, although it is one of its defining components. As John Tomlinson remarks, "We must remember that the discourses of cultural imperialism as media imperialism or as the attack on national cultural identity or, here, as the spread across the globe of a culture of capitalism do not 'totalise' to a coherent thesis. They are 'ways of talking' about processes which have been loosely and sometimes contradictorily 'organised' by the concept 'cultural imperialism'" (102).

7. Genet's inscription of himself as the narrator of his texts is certainly akin to postmodernist auto-bio-graphy where, in Brian McHale's terms, "the supposedly absolute reality of the author becomes just another level of fiction, and the real world retreats to a further remove" (197).

8. This doubling effect is a constant throughout Genet's novels and has received ample treatment by critics. For the most part, Genet's treatment of the double has been interpreted as a primarily existential problem, a process of metamorphosis in which the self becomes other to trace out being as an endless pursuit of illusion. See, for example, Gerald Storzer's "The Homosexual Paradigm in Balzac, Gide and Genet" and Laura Oswald's *The Semiotics of Performance* for pertinent discussions based on this perspective. The argument I am advancing here—namely that the centrality of doubling in Genet's work can be linked to the impact of the mechanically reproduced image on subjectivity—has yet to be explored in Genet's work from the perspective of the function of the image.

9. Jerry Aline Flieger examines Genet's *Notre-Dame-des-fleurs* in relation to dreamwork and jokes. Drawing on Freudian theory, Fleiger argues that Genet's "piecemeal recomposition of character, decor, and situation from fragments of real life, a sort of collage which is the prevailing stylistic technique in the work, is clearly analogous to the dreamwork technique of displacement, in which dream elements are moved around and rearranged in order to elude censorship" (73). Flieger's thoughtful analysis does not consider the specific role (media) images play in creating this effect which, in the terms of my argument, is that of the hyperreal.

10. Various critics have drawn attention to Genet's use of cinematic techniques such as collage and montage in his novels although for the most part, systematic studies of Genet and the cinema are undertaken in reference to Genet's one fully realized film—*Un Chant d'amour* (1950)—and his other film

scenarios—*La Révolte des anges noirs* (1947), *Le Bagne* ('50s), *Les Rêves interdits, ou L'Autre Versant du rêve* (ca. 1952), *Le Bleu de l'œil/La Nuit venue* (1976–1978), and *Le Langage de la muraille* ('60s).

11. Steven Shaviro's theorization of the cinematic gaze in *The Cinematic Body* is grounded in the spectator's experience of shock and fascination in view of images. Taking into consideration the speed with which cinematic images excite the retina, Shaviro formulates a model of spectatorship based on powerlessness: "I do not have power over what I see, I do not even have, strictly speaking, the power to see; it is more that I am powerless not to see. The darkness of the movie theater isolates me from the rest of the audience, and cuts off any possibility of 'normal' perception. I cannot willfully focus my attention on this or on that. Instead, my gaze is arrested by the sole area of light, a flux of moving images. I am attentive to what happens on the screen only to the extent that I am continually distracted, and passively absorbed by it" (48). I find this model of viewing images useful insofar as it postulates a loosening of fixed identities and subjectivity as a primary effect.

12. The juxtaposition of the feudal age with the contemporary age that one finds throughout Genet's novels can thus be described as an effect of the image on the author-narrator's sense of time and space.

13. See for example, Jerry Aline Flieger's "Dream, Humor and Power in Genet's *Notre-Dame-des-fleurs*," Frederick J. Harris's "Linguistic Reality—Historical Reality: Genet, Céline, Grass," and David Walker's "Antecedents for Genet's Persona."

14. This can explain why Genet's most beloved images are of criminals who have been either condemned to death (such as Harcamone or Weidmann) or already executed (such as Pilorge).

15. Indeed, the characters in Genet's novels spring directly from the author-narrator's fascination with images he clips from the newspapers, or sees on the cover of pulp fiction novels or at the movies. *Notre-Dame-des-fleurs*, for example, is written "[à] l'aide de mes amants inconnus" (16), "une vingtaine de photographies" (14). Significantly, facing these images, which serve as the heros of the story, the narrator becomes one of them, that is an image among images, an empty site or spectral subject serving only to recount the birth and death of further images to come. As the narrator describes, "Sourires et moues, les uns et les autres inexorables, m'entrent par tous mes trous offerts, leur vigueur pénètre en moi et m'érige. Je vis parmi ces gouffres. Ils président à

mes petites habitudes, qui sont, avec eux, toute ma famille et mes seuls amis" (14).

16 "Of whoever is fascinated it can be said that he dosen't perceive any real object, any real figure, for what he sees does not belong to the world of reality, but to the indeterminate milieu of fascination" (Blanchot, *Space* 32).

17. As Susan Sontag notes in her article "Fascinating Fascism," "There is a general fantasy about uniforms. They suggest community, order, identity (through ranks, badges, medals, things which delcare who the wearer is and what he has done: his worth is recognized), competence, legitimate authority, the legitimate exercise of violence. But uniforms are not the same thing as photographs of uniforms—which are erotic materials and photographs of SS uniforms are the units of a particularly powerful and widespread sexual fantasy" (*Under the Sign of Saturn* 99).

18. Ella Shohat and Robert Stam address this central issue in their chapter "Multiculturalism in the Postmodern Age." See especially pp. 342–47.

19. For a more lengthy discussion of history in postmodernist fiction, see Brian McHale's chapter "Real, Compared to What?" in *Postmodernist Fiction*, pp. 84–96.

20. As Baudrillard explains in *Symbolic Exchange and Death*, cannibals live in a society that eats its own dead "neither due to a vital necessity nor because the dead no longer count for anything, quite the contrary: it is in order to pay homage to them…. This devouring is a social act, a *symbolic* act, that aims to maintain a tissue of bonds with the dead man or the enemy they devour. In any case they don't just eat anybody, as we know; whoever is eaten is always somebody worthy, it is always a mark of respect to devour somebody since, through this, the devoured even becomes sacred…. Neither the fulfillment of desire nor the assimilation of something or other, it is on the contrary an act of expenditure, consumption or consummation, and of the transmutation of the flesh into a symbolic relation, the transformation of the body in social exchange" (138, emphasis in original).

21. Nathalie Fredette's article "Jean Genet: les pouvoirs de l'imposture" specifically addresses the multiple positions of the bodies in *Pompes funèbres* in relation to the political subject.

22. Shohat and Stam discuss the ambiguity inherent in the media. Commenting upon the fact that spectatorship is not *necessarily* regressive, they write: "Media

spectatorship forms a trialog between texts, readers, and communitites existing in clear discursive and social relation to one another. It is thus a negotiable site of interaction and struggle, seen, for example, in the possibility of 'aberrant' or resistant readings, as the consciousness or experience of a particular audience generates a counter-pressure to dominant representations" (347).

23. The continuity between the various audiences is further underscored in *Pompes funèbres* by the recurrence of a female spectator who serves a similar function in each scene: to comment on the spectacle she is viewing and, in turn, to project the voice of the nation. That Genet chooses to voice national hypocrisy and/or collaboration through female spectators underscores the "feminization" undergone by France in its collaboration with Germany, a recurrent metaphor in French writings at the time. However, it also draws (uncritically) upon a whole register of negative imagery associated with femininity and female sexuality in order to figure the nation as a diseased body.

24. In effect, this cinematic experience, by tying the initial sequences of the novel together, thus contextualizes the remainder of the novel within the film, thereby blurring the presentation of historical fact with fiction and allowing the author-narrator a critical space within which to take up the identities presented on screen. In taking up these identities, Genet articulates a vision of this critical moment in history from a plurality of voices, voices that alternately contradict and reaffirm each other. Genet's use of the movies in *Pompes funèbres* is comparable in this sense to the use of television and movies in postmodernist fiction. As Brian McHale points out, "Instead of serving as a repertoire of representational techniques, the movies and television appear in postmodernist writing as an ontological level: a world-within-the-world, often one in competition with the primary diagetic world of the text, or a plane interposed between the level of verbal representation and the level of the 'real'" (128).

25. Laura Oswald attributes the shifting of identities in *Pompes funèbres* to the figure of the mask. Her analysis, which accounts for the narrator's transformations into his characters, does not consider, however, the role media images play in creating the performative context, nor does it discuss the centrality of media images to the blurring of the lines between the real and the fake.

26. Umberto Eco describes the place of the individual in "Ur-Fascism" in his article "Fourteen ways of looking at a blackshirt:" "For Ur-Fascism...individuals as individuals have no rights, and the People is conceived as a quality, a monolithic entity expressing the Common Will." Genet's description of the "masse armée" in *Pompes funèbres* resembles this characterization.

27. As John Tomlinson explains, "National identities are not cultural belongings rooted in deep quasi-natural attachments to a homeland, but, rather, complex cultural constructions that have arisen in specific historical conditions [those of modernity]. There is a 'lived reality' of national identity, but it is a reality lived in representations" (84). Cinema, moreover, has proven to be a privileged medium for the relaying of the "projected narratives" of nations, for as Shohat and Stam suggest, "The cinema's institutionalized ritual of gathering a community—spectators who share a region, language, and culture— homologizes, in a sense, the symbolic gathering of the nation" (103).

28. In this sense, it could be said that Genet establishes a subversive intertext with Jules Michelet who, as Benedict Anderson explains, was among the first historians to exhume the dead and speak on their behalf for the benefits of national history: "Michelet made it clear that those whom he was exhuming were by no means a random assemblage of forgotten, anonymous dead. They were those whose sacrifices, throughout History, made possible the rupture of 1789 and the selfconscious appearance of the French nation, *even when these sacrifices were not understood as such by the victims....* Michelet not only claimed to speak on behalf of large numbers of anonymous dead people, but insisted, with poignant authority, that he could say what they 'really' meant and 'really' wanted, since they themselves 'did not understand.' From then on, the silence of the dead was no obstacle to the exhumation of their deepest desires" (198).

29. For as Genet points out to Roger Blin, "If we maintain that life and the stage are opposites, it is because we strongly suspect that the stage is a site closely akin to death, a place where all liberties are possible" (*Reflections* 12).

30. See David Bradby's "Genet, the Theatre and the Algerian War." It is important to note that although the context of the play is evident, Genet never mentions Algeria specifically in the play.

31. I recall here Genet's famous formulation which links theatricality to power. Speaking about the events of May '68, Genet remarks, "Finalement, les étudiants ont occupé un théâtre. Qu'est-ce que c'est qu'un théâtre? D'abord qu'est-ce que c'est que le pouvoir? Il me semble que le pouvoir ne peut se passer de théâtralité. Jamais. La théâtralité est quelquefois simplifiée, elle est quelquefois changée mais il y a toujours théâtralité. Le pouvoir se met à l'abri d'une théâtralité, en Chine, en Union soviétique, en Angleterre, en France, partout, c'est la théâtralité qui domine.... Il y a un endroit au monde où la théâtralité ne cache aucun pouvoir, c'est le théâtre" (*Dialogues* 24).

32. As Shohat and Stam explain, "Although colonialist discourse and Eurocentric discourse are intimately intertwined, the terms have a distinct emphasis. While

the former explicitly justifies colonialist practices, the latter embeds, takes for granted, and 'normalizes' the hierarchical power relations generated by colonialism and imperialism, without necessarily even thematizing those issues directly. Although generated by the colonizing process, Eurocentrism's links to that process are obscured in a kind of buried epistemology" (2). For a discussion on the distinction between imperialism and globalization, see also John Tomlinson's conclusion "From Imperialism to Globalisation," especially p. 175.

3 | Hervé Guibert: Writing the Spectral Image

Les phrases sont la nourriture et elles sont les monuments des morts, elles sont leurs oeuvres, leurs romans...

—*Hervé Guibert*

There are no remote places. Under instant circuitry, nothing is remote in time or in space. It's now.

—*Marshall McLuhan*

It would be hard to find a writer more immersed in contemporary image culture than Hervé Guibert. Some would even say, alongside Françoise Giroud, that "Guibert est né du ventre de la télévision" (31). For as Giroud and others have pointed out, despite the fact that Guibert had written twenty-six works ranging from poetry and prose to film scenarios and theatre, it was only after the publication of his first AIDS narrative—*A l'ami qui ne m'a pas sauvé la vie* (1990)—and his television appearance on France's literary talk show *Apostrophes* that Guibert first gained notoriety in the public eye—not as a writer, but as a gay writer dying with and writing about AIDS. Since that moment, Guibert's life and work have drawn considerable attention (his T.V. appearance had made him an overnight success) not only because of his direct and personal testimony of life with AIDS (so rare among French artists and writers) but also because of the fictionalized presence throughout Guibert's post-AIDS texts of one of France's most enigmatic thinkers, Michel Foucault.[1]

Having associated Foucault with sado-masochistic sexuality and (the intentional spread of) AIDS in his later, seemingly autobiographical work, Guibert has indeed been charged with betraying the privacy so carefully cultivated by the "masked philosopher," who was also one of his dearest friends. And Foucault is not the only "celebrity" to make an appearance in Guibert's work shrouded by scandal.[2] In effect, Guibert transplants real-world persons in the form of (barely) fictionalized characters throughout his novels which, in turn, are presented as autobiographical accounts that aim to, in the author's words, "réduire cette distance entre les vérités de l'expérience et de l'écriture" (qtd. in Boulé, "Introduction" 2). What are we, the readers, to make of this migration?[3] For some, Guibert's writing project is accepted at face value: an exercise in pure narcissism. Not only does he reveal the secrets of close friends and family but, like Thomas Mann's later diaries, his novels are somewhat shocking in their sexual and medical specificity. Moreover, they contain "a mass of trivia which at first appear to have no *raison d'être* other than the author's narcissistic sense of importance" (Vaget 567). These elements, combined with the sensationalistic manner in which Guibert was "discovered," could certainly lead us to position Guibert within "the society of the spectacle" or the "culture of narcissism"—that is to say a new politics of voyeurism and exhibitionism that falls under the sign of commodity culture and the ethical code of mass marketing. Drawing as it does on personal experience and confession, Guibert's mode of writing is easily construed as belonging to exhibitionism, which itself has fast become a growth industry in the eighties and nineties.[4] Michael Worton's description of Guibert's writing project, taken from *French Cultural Studies: An Introduction* (1995) edited by Jill Forbes and Michael Kelly, is, I believe, representative of this perception. Worton writes:

> Although he was reluctant to use the term autobiography, Guibert himself is present in most of his works—as are members of his family.... Furthermore, Guibert often included evocations of his friends in his works: there is, for example, a cruel portrait of Gina Lollobrigida in *Les Aventures singulières* (1982) and, most famously, a portrait of Foucault...in *A l'ami qui ne m'a pas sauvé la vie* (1990). Guibert's revelations of Foucault's innermost secrets surprised and shocked many people, especially since Foucault normally talked very little in public about his family, his childhood, or his sexual life, and had indeed argued for years against the imperative to tell the truth and the duty to confess.... Guibert is

astonishly narcissistic and his autobiographical fictions are often spiteful and threaded through with betrayals of those who have cared for him... (206)

Reading Guibert's work, it is difficult to deny the scandalous pleasures it holds.[5] Can we therefore assume that Guibert effectively "sold out" in choosing to fictionalize his relationship with Foucault and other celebrities? Were it not for his writing about AIDS, would Guibert have "made it" into the literary limelight (symbolized by the tele-vision of *Apostrophes*)? And what does Guibert's example tell us about the conditions of possibility for writers and literature in the information age?

In an "infomercial" culture such as ours, where the "theater of public confession" has the power to pathologize society at large,[6] writers have certainly not remained impervious. After all, as Stephen Heath remarks, "[l]iterature today is a massive accelerated production, coming and going every week" (1058). With literary talk shows such as *Apostrophes* setting the standard of "reading for pleasure,"

> [w]hat is important is the spectacle of the author and the creation before our eyes of his or her book as 'the book of the author,' in the same way that we talk of 'the book of the film:' something to which we are subsequently incited and which gains its impact from its reactivation of what we first saw, the true substance. No longer dead, the author has now become the very condition of the book's reality, its television life. (Heath 1055)

In Guibert's case, as we have seen, moving beyond the author-as-spectacle is extremely difficult. Due to the relationship he establishes throughout his texts between personal experience and the act of writing/representation, it is quite tempting, as Raymond Bellour has warned, to reduce Guibert's writing to the display value of the confession.[7] However, as I will discuss below, to (mis)read as truth the "secrets" divulged in Guibert's novels, or to take seriously his portrayals of famous artists, actors, and intellectuals, is also to discount the primacy of the experimental and the experiential in Guibert's aesthetic, *especially* where truth and self-representation are concerned.[8] It is also to succumb, perhaps unwittingly, to the lure of the simulacrum so prevalent in contemporary image culture. In effect, by means of a documentary and/or quasi-photographic gaze, Guibert's writing hovers in the realm between reality and fiction, a dynamic we can associate with the larger cultural context of images today. From this perspective, as we have been discussing throughout this study, the status of both *truth* and experience remains elusive. It is precisely upon this paradox, I contend, that Guibert's literary enterprise is built.

My aim in this chapter, then, is to examine the relationship between Guibert's literary aesthetic (his declared mode to "tout dire" in writing)[9] and contemporary image culture. I will begin first by looking at the mediation of personal experience through image technologies from a broad cultural perspective in order to provide a basis by which to contextualize Guibert's aesthetic within the "society of the spectacle" and its hyperreal atmosphere. This vantage point will enable us to see that Guibert builds his texts around the ambiguity of the image towards the creation of a new literary genre, one that is in close dialogue with contemporary consumer practices.

My discussion will then focus on three texts by Guibert which establish an intimate connection between the image, death, and self identity (i.e. the experience of one's self/body): *L'Image fantôme, Mon Valet et moi*, and *L'Homme au chapeau rouge*. We will see that if, for Guibert, images derealize death, leaving in its place a morbid voyeurism and a certain bloodlust that has taken hold over consumers' imaginations, images nevertheless are also what sustain our relationship to it. Guibert's practice of writing is therefore synchronous with his practice of the image, both of which work toward (re)opening the image up to its most profound origin: death.

Emotional Exhibitionism: Personal Experience in the Postmodern "Scanscape"

Faced with the collapse of public and private spheres operated by the increasing mediatization of life in technoculture, personal experience today often translates into that which has been, or can be, filmed. Indeed, as cameras proliferate, surveying and recording everything from the moon and the stars to foreign parts of the world and even the routine activities of our own daily lives (security cameras in shopping malls, banks, schools, etc.), new forms of public entertainment based on reportage and testimonials filmed in real life situations have taken hold over the public's imagination. These forms of entertainment, or "reality voyeurism" as Kevin Robins aptly calls them, range from television reality shows to vigilante documentation to webcams.[10] Their appeal, similar to that of more traditional media such as radio and the popular press, stems from their ability to involve the viewers emotionally and provide them with a sense of community. As Pierre Sorlin suggests, media "illustrate a way of life familiar to many of their clients and provide some of them with a chance to participate in an active, committed cycle of exchanges" (66).[11] Robins, in his discussion of contemporary image technologies, also underscores the media's appeal to viewer participation and emotional investment in a simulated community experience; within the world of reality television, made up of the city streets, neighborhoods and homes,

> [v]iewers watch themselves, their neighbours and the strangers and aliens that surround them. Ordinary people are its stars, and frequently it is they who have produced its images. It is a television of misfortunes, disasters and crimes that afflict urban life. But also a television of how ordinary people cope with and survive them, everyday heroes of the urban scene. Reality television is a kind of morality television, publicising the private and intimate lives of its viewers in order to help them to deal with the complexities and contingencies of the perilous city. (140)

The media, as Pierre Sorlin observes, have always been vehicles of sociability, helping people to make sense of the world in which they live and satisfying a desire to observe other people. However, as Susan Bordo remarks, now that "our consumer culture has developed a virtual science of image making and illusion creating," it has become "frighteningly adept at technologically manipulating elements to form seemingly unaltered new wholes" (91). Locating any reality outside the realm of created images today, much less a meaningful "sense of the world" referred to above by Sorlin, is an extremely dubious undertaking at best. In effect, having cast aside notions of truth and reality in favor of simulacra, spectators today, according to Baudrillard, are caught up in the frenetic pace of the "après orgie." This phase, which he also calls the fractal age, establishes the absence of distinction between values, ideology and signs:

> L'orgie, c'est tout le moment explosif de la modernité, celui de la libération dans tous les domaines…. Ce fut une orgie totale, de réel, de rationnel, de sexuel, de critique, et d'anti-critique, de croissance et de crise de croissance. Nous avons parcouru tous les chemins de la production et de la surproduction virtuelle d'objets, de signes, de messages, d'idéologies, de plaisirs. Aujourd'hui, tout est libéré, les jeux sont faits, et nous nous retrouvons collectivement devant la question cruciale: QUE FAIRE APRES L'ORGIE ? (*La Transparence du mal* 11)

We are thus "stuck" in simulation; a state whereby we imitate movement in the same direction as before, only at an accelerated pace and in an orgiastic manner. However, we are accelerating in a void (of a completed liberation), merely simulating scenarios that have already occured—"réellement ou virtuellement." It is at this stage—"l'utopie réalisée"—that Baudrillard introduces his notion of the hyperreal: "la reproduction indéfinie d'idéaux, de fantasmes, d'images, de rêves qui sont désormais derrière nous, et qu'il nous faut cependant reproduire dans une sorte d'indifférence fatale" (12). This indifferent reproduction of images, as Baudrillard explains, leads to an implosion of the image and the real so that, ultimately, we are no longer able to (nor do we *want* to) distinguish between the two.[12] In this sense, images have no finality, they are no more than object-fetishes that, far from representing any reality, reproduce only more images. Images, then, become more real than the real and operate within their own logic, thus leaving behind the world of signification and propelling bodies into a hyperspace where they lose all meaning. Hervé Guibert's description of "la retoucheuse" from *L'Image fantôme*, a book composed of various tableaux which explore different types of images, aptly illustrates the hyperreal:

> Entre les agences de publicité, les médias et les consommateurs, les retoucheurs font figure d'agents secrets, d'exécuteurs obscurs et innommables, de grands exterminateurs de l'imperfection. La retoucheuse déblaye et embellit la réalité. Mais elle est aussi un peu une magicienne:

elle peut faire voler les avions au repos, mettre des cheveux sur les crânes chauves pour les publicités de lotions contre la calvitie. Elle peut fermer des yeux ouverts et rouvrir des yeux fermés, elle peut faire marcher les morts. (139)

In this slippery postmodern terrain, where our sense of reality is forged by image technologies, there has been a breakdown of ideas about what constitutes objective reality and universal truth, thereby opening a chasm in the ways we interpret events in the world and paving the way for what some have called emotional exhibitionism.[13] Indeed, lacking any universal basis (or metanarrative) upon which to achieve critical distance, people are turning their backs on reason in favor of feelings and sensations. As François Brune explains:

> On the one hand, there is a world that can no longer be understood or mastered, and, on the other, there is the primacy of the visual and of its euphoric and dramatised signs…. The substitutes of image and emotion are offered to those who have lost hold on the real world. (qtd. in Robins 121)

Guibert's texts, as we discussed above, appeal to this consumer fantasy of emotional experience at a distance in their disclosure of explicit details about his intimate life with family and friends.[14] Moreover, his texts also exude an aura of sensationalism. Yet, if Guibert positions his aesthetic on the side of "reality voyeurism" or the hyperreal, it is not to disavow real experience in favor of simulation, as is commonly the case with consumers today.[15] To the contrary, Guibert incorporates image and vision technologies into his mode of writing as a means to scrutinize the ways in which they affect both perception and experience, altering in the process not only the epistemological resources of our culture, but also its subjective, bodily, and other experiential dimensions—especially death. The projection of home movies described by the narrator in *L'Image fantôme*, for example, sollicits a combination of emotions from the family viewers that range from nostalgia to fear and finally to desire. This sequence also demonstrates the extent to which images at once connect us to death, yet at the same time elicit defensive reactions to it. As the narrator observes:

Cette projection a donné lieu à une révision nostalgique; cela devait faire dix ans qu'on n'avait pas fait marcher le projecteur, mais c'était peut-être la dernière fois qu'on le faisait marcher. La nervosité de ma mère redoublait—peut-être la peur de se revoir jeune—, et s'exprimait par des inquiétudes détournées et idiotes ('c'est le transfo qui sent. Arrête, on va mettre le feu'). Les films sont muets et il m'intéressait de voir de quels sous-titres on allait les agrémenter, quel discours familial pouvait se greffer sur ces images. En relevant des phrases de-ci de-là qui échappaient au babillage descriptif, j'ai pu me rendre compte à quel point ce discours était angoissé et porteur de mort. J'en retranscris ici quelques-unes, dans l'ordre:

—Il s'est suicidé Robert...

—Il a eu les jambes coupées Edouard...

—Il y a beaucoup de gens mort là-dedans... (48–49)

Through the blurring of the lines between real life experience and the experience of images, Guibert's texts position themselves within an overall shift in audiovisual culture—embodying it as well as commenting on it—where the image, rather than the flesh and blood body of the Other, is what provides our points of contact both with the world and with ourselves. Through his photographic writing, as we will explore below, Guibert superposes life experience onto the factual evidence of images in order to highlight the complexity of perception, subjectivity, and truth in contemporary image culture. In the end, as the following example from *L'Image fantôme* demonstrates, even when we seem to be participating with Guibert in his most intimate and revealing moments, the subject behind the autobiographical mask evades our attempts to know his truth, leaving us haunted by an enigmatic spectral image or a Blanchotian cadaverous presence whose identity will forever remain deferred:

Il y a quelques années, j'ai fixé sur la vitre de la porte-fenêtre qui fait face à ma table de travail une radiographie, retrouvée par hasard dans la chemise d'un carton à dessin, d'un profil gauche de mon torse pris le 20 avril 1972, à l'âge de dix-sept ans. La lumière passe au travers de cet enchevêtrement bleuté de lignes osseuses et de flous d'organes comme au travers d'un vitrail, mais surtout en affichant là, et à la vue de tous (des voisins comme des visiteurs), cette radiographie, je placarde l'image la plus intime de moi-même, bien plus qu'un nu, celle qui renferme l'énigme, et qu'un étudiant en médecine pourrait facilement déchiffrer. Je n'ai plus chez moi aucune photo de moi, cela m'horripile chez les autres, mais j'affiche là, avec un plaisir d'exhibitionniste, l'image d'une différence de base... (68)

Like the subject of telecommunications according to Guillaume, the subject in *L'Image fantôme* thus suspends traditional notions of identity to float in the space of projection from which it is screened—despite the statistical fixity of its presentation ("un profil gauche de mon torse pris le 20 avril 1972, à l'âge de dix-sept ans").

Photographic Writing and Autobiography

Like Roland Barthes in *Camera Lucida* (1981), Hervé Guibert explores the sensual and affective dimensions of photography throughout his work: he is concerned not with its rationalistic or artistic/aesthetic uses, but rather with the ways in which photography moves him and figures into his bodily and emotional experience.[16] What is at stake in this approach to photography is the relationship between perception (the seer) and truth (the seen), as well as the role of the photograph as a mediator of truth.

John Berger, among others, has pointed out how the photograph has been generally associated with the "utter truth" due to its status of fact. Indeed, the truthfulness of the photograph is assumed to be the same in widely different contexts: when used scientifically, photographs provide evidence and information; when used in a control system, such as that of public communication, their evidence establishes identity and presence (*Another Way of Telling* 98). Yet, as Berger further explains, when lived experience is involved, one risks confusing very different levels of the truth. "[As] soon as a photograph is used as a means of communication," he writes,

> the nature of lived experience is involved, and then the truth becomes more complex. An X-ray photograph of a wounded leg can tell the 'utter truth' about whether the bones are fractured or not. But how does a photograph tell the 'utter truth' about a man's experience of hunger or, for that matter, his experience of a feast? (*Another Way* 98)

Thus is the ambiguity of the photograph: capable of showing our bodies even to the point where the invisible becomes the visible, as in Guibert's X-ray of his torso, photographic images nevertheless always remain enigmatic—they cannot, in and of themselves, tell us the truth about ourselves. As Berger succinctly remarks, "...the photograph cannot lie, but, by the same token, it cannot tell the truth; or rather, the truth it does tell, the truth it can by itself defend, is a limited one" (*Another Way* 97).

In the global system of late capitalism, however, the innate ambiguity of the photograph is lost, sacrificed to the market where images function not to communicate experience, but rather to create experience as a commodity. In other words, in technoculture, images configure the individual consumer's dream which, in its turn, comes to stand for that individual's model of life experience. For Berger, it is precisely this commodification of experience that leads to the denial of the social function of subjectivity and the *repli sur soi* we have been discussing, for in such a system,

> [a]ll subjectivity is treated as private, and the only (false) form of it which is socially allowed is that of the individual consumer's dream. From this primary suppression of the social function of subjectivity, other suppressions follow: of meaningful democracy (replaced by opinion polls and market-research techniques), of social conscience (replaced by self-interest), of history (replaced by racist and other myths), of hope—the most subjective and social of all energies (replaced by the sacralisation of Progress as Comfort). (*Another Way* 100)

Seizing upon the ambiguity particular to the image, Hervé Guibert successfully transformed it into a practice of writing-the-self that has been described by critics as the creation of a new literary genre. Called "le roman faux" by Jean-Pierre Boulé (4) and "la conception d'un fantastique de soi-même" by Raymond Bellour (121), Guibert's new genre anchors itself precisely in the ontological flicker provoked by image technologies and the space of the screen.[17] Guibert's writing of the self—his autoportrait—is in constant flux between the true and the false, for, as he specifies, it is precisely at the point where these two postulates meet and masquerade as each other that they acquire meaning:

Ce qui m'intéresse le plus c'est la façon dont c'est tramé; le documentaire et la fantasmagorie à la fois allant de pair et se trompant l'un l'autre. Parfois, là où l'on croit à la fantasmagorie, c'est du documentaire, et là où on peut croire à du documentaire, c'est une pure affabulation que la vérité démentirait. (qtd. in Smyth 12)

What interests Guibert in his avowed project to "tout dire" in writing, both about himself and his family and friends, is thus not associated with any fixed (verifiable) truths or the doctrine of self-expression. Rather, as Bellour aptly describes, "…l'essentiel se joue, à partir de la confession et *de ses apparences*, sur un autre terrain… [Guibert] a toujours gardé les yeux fixes sur le point à partir duquel une vie se transforme en livre" (121, my emphasis).[18]

If Hervé Guibert positions the image at the center of his intimate sensations and subjective experience, therefore, it is not because this medium offers complete and truthful knowledge of himself to his readers. To the contrary, *against* the grain of these commercial uses of photography and vision technologies, Guibert's practice of the image is concerned with the condition of (self)knowledge in the space of the screen, and the transformation of experience this space entails. More specifically, he focuses on the image's connections to death and disaster and uses them to explore our culture's simultaneous attraction to—and distanciation from—the real experience of death. Since Guibert chronicles his own experience of dying with AIDS in his later texts, it is tempting to consider the whole of his work through this (autobiographical) optic.[19] Yet, as he points out in his first AIDS narrative, *A l'ami qui ne m'a pas sauvé la vie*, this virus only furthered the relationship established early on for him between death and the image, a relationship that shaped Guibert's approach not only to dying, but also to fiction:[20]

Depuis que j'ai douze ans, et depuis qu'elle est une terreur, la mort est une marotte. J'en ignorais l'existence jusqu'à ce qu'un camarade de classe, le petit Bonnecarère, m'envoyât au cinéma le Styx, où l'on s'asseyait à l'époque dans des cercueils, voir *L'enterré vivant*, un film de Roger Corman tiré d'un conte d'Edgar Allan Poe. La découverte de la mort par le truchement de cette vision horrifique…devint une source capiteuse de cauchemars. Par la suite, je ne cessai de rechercher les attributs les plus spectaculaires de la mort…m'hypnotisant de films d'épouvante et commençant à écrire, sous le pseudonyme d'Hector Lenoir, un conte qui racontait les affres d'un fantôme enchaîné dans les oubliettes du château des Hohenzollern, me grisant de lectures macabres…errant dans les cimetières et étrennant mon premier appareil avec des photographies de tombes d'enfants…la mort me semblait horriblement belle, féeriquement atroce…comme imprégné par elle au plus profond…je continuais inlassablement de quérir son sentiment, le plus précieux et le plus haïssable d'entre tous, sa peur et sa convoitise. (150)

This image of a young Guibert sitting in a coffin discovering violence, suffering, and death through a horror film, as well as his subsequent fascination with death's pull on the imagination which leads him to actively seek out its most spectacular manifestations, are testimony to the derealization and exclusion of real death in our culture. It is as if the sofas in our living rooms and the seats in our movie theaters have transformed themselves into the modern version of the cemetery, for it is only in front of the (television/movie) screen that we entertain a relationship with death.[21] If cemeteries have long been a rich source of information about a culture's ideas, past and present, of community, this form of knowing the past is undergoing rapid changes at the *fin de siècle* due to cultural changes imported by image technologies. Eleanor Weinel, for example, draws out the impact of society's attitude toward the body, experience, and memory in the elimination of cemeteries. "Having detached ourselves from the importance of corporeal reality in death and the related rituals of maintenance," she writes,

we also have relinquished our conceptual link to the final resting place as a site of individual and collective memory. Our means of memory are too many and too real to require the aid of monuments and the emotions they elicit. Video tape, with its illusion of reality, supplants recollection in the private as well as the public sphere. (50)

Fully aware that literature may be the final resting place of the dead for future generations, perhaps its *only* remaining memorial, Guibert incorporates the technical operations of photography and video into his work and transforms them into a face-to-face confrontation with death. Throughout the remainder of this chapter, I will focus more specifically on the extent to which Guibert draws on the "contaminating" quality of the image to represent this confrontation, and the ways in which he subverts consumer society's denial of the body and experience in its obsessive screening of violent images.

In a time when the culture of virtual reality is enabling an escape from the anxieties of the real world through its appeal to the disembodied pleasures of consumption, Guibert brings the image back in touch with the body and subjective experience. In so doing, he exposes the illusory (and dangerous) nature of a system that professes to have liberated people even from their own deaths.

Spectral Images

Hervé Guibert's death on December 27, 1991 put an end to his writing project that had consisted of transcribing his experience into writing through a language that approximated the instantaneousness of the photograph. Indeed, through his photographic writing, which he describes in *L'Image fantôme* as "la trace la plus récente de la mémoire, et c'est à peine de la mémoire: comme quelque chose qui semble encore vibrer sur la rétine, c'est de l'impression, presque de l'instantané" (75), Guibert sought to come into direct contact with his readers, to communicate with them via a certain hypervision. From within this experimental state, where image technologies and the media blur the boundaries between inside and outside, self and other, information circulates in what has been referred to by Baudrillard and others as a viral mode. Guibert, who takes the communicable elements of information quite literally, endows media and its vehicles (i.e. photography) with the power to imprint themselves onto bodies, engendering in the process the spread of infectious disease:

> Ce n'est pas ma veine: j'attrape tout ce que je touche, tout ce que je lis existe. C'est en lisant les journaux que j'ai contracté le sida. Je suis immuno-déficitaire. Puisque ma peau a touché des vêtements qui recouvraient la peau du Gitan couverte de taches blanches de dépigmentation, son tee-shirt imbibé va les décalquer sur la mienne comme un négatif photographique. Je suis positif, très sensible en ce qui concerne la reproduction. (*L'Incognito* 222)

Drawing on parallels between the spread of information and its colonization of reality and the spread of AIDS and its colonization of the body, Guibert's success and talent as a writer could very well lie in his ability to turn AIDS into a process of creative generation rather than destruction, one that is intricately linked to the central current of the postmodern debate: the image.[22] As we shall see, the experience of AIDS becomes, like photography, the medium by which Guibert's images fuse reality and fiction, thus generating a constellation of images that compose the hyperreal body. In Guibert's *L'Homme au chapeau rouge*, the body-with-AIDS is a privileged site from which the text radiates, much like a virus. In *Mon Valet et moi*, the viral, contaminating quality of images "infects" the narrator's body as well as his subjectivity, leading him to a certain paranoia. Significantly, this viral proliferation is at once a component of AIDS and a component of the image, as Jacques Henric has already implied:

> L'animal humain est, lui aussi, malade de la peste. D'une étrange peste. A la différence de ce qui se passe pour les autres organismes vivants, il ne s'agit pas d'une épidémie passagère, d'une éruption violente, meurtrière mais néanmoins combattable, jugulable, circonscrivable. Si elle présente, elle aussi, ses moments nettement ravageurs, ses points d'intense fièvre dévastatrice, cette peste-là, dont je parle, a la particularité d'être invincible. Son feu ne cesse de couver sous la cendre. Il suffit d'un rien...—le déconnage de quelques cellules qui, ayant tâté de l'anarchie, se mettent à faire sans frein des petits—pour que le mal recommence à souffler par rafales.... Cette peste très speciale, immémoriale, irréductible, porte un nom: l'*image*. (184)

The similitude between the image (as plague) and AIDS is not surprising, considering that the postmodern era seems to be caracterized by both "viruses."[23] In fact, both the image and AIDS function according to the same process. In much the same way that the HIV virus invades the cellular system, concurrently disturbing its replication and contaminating it, the image, in Baudrillard's sense, reproduces the real in a viral manner:[24]

> en tant que simulacre, l'image précède le réel dans la mesure où elle inverse la succession logique, causale, du réel et de sa reproduction... L'image est intéressante quand elle commence à contaminer le réel et à le 'modéliser,' quand elle ne se conforme au réel que pour mieux le

déformer, mieux: quand elle subtilise le réel à son profit, quand elle anticipe sur lui au point que le réel n'a plus le temps de se produire en tant que tel. ("Au delà" 157)

Hervé Guibert's work is an exemplary model of fiction "contaminated" by the "real." The deformation of the real by images is a recurrent motif in his novels, and, as we discussed above, constitutes a central element of his vision as a writer of the postmodern era. Indeed, his *L'Image fantôme* is a text entirely dedicated to the malefic power of images. The narrator of *L'Image fantôme* emphasizes the negative influence images can have in our daily lives by introducing us to the problematic via so-called autobiographical elements, such as photographs and home movies. In the example below, the narrator's parents demonstrate that the act of watching a home movie is no longer a simple routine of the traditional family. The parents, as they watch the movie, are transformed into opaque signs as they are confronted with the image of their younger bodies on film. The bodies, as a result of a violent love/hate relationship to the image, wish at once to fuse with the images and to destroy them. In this way, the reality of the moment spent watching the film is contaminated by the presence of what the narrator calls "ces vilains mirages, ces trop beaux mirages." The Baudelairean pastiche here overcodes the act of writing as a process of assembling ghostly images:[25]

> Nos corps nous sont maintenant insensibles, invisibles, et nous aimons secrètement et nous haïssons en même temps ces corps jeunes qui passent comme des fantômes dans le pinceau lumineux du projecteur. Nous les aimons au point de désirer, par une magie inverse, entrer dans l'image, et l'étreindre, revenir avec elle dans le passé, nous les haïssons au point de vouloir les défigurer, les mutiler, les rayer à la pointe d'une aiguille à même le film, pour qu'ils ne nous narguent plus, ces vilains mirages, ces trop beaux mirages. (*L'Image* 52)

L'Image fantôme reveals some central components of Guibert's conceptualization of images, especially in their relationship to the homoerotic body: the images bear elements of masochism and they fuse death with life. Here we encounter the spectral image, an image born of the intersections and interchangeability of life (reality), death (images), and writing. In other words, the spectral image replicates a clone. It is the dying (homoerotic) body-of-writing (a body composed of writing):

> Le texte n'aurait pas été si l'image avait été prise. L'image serait là devant moi, probablement encadrée, parfaite et fausse, irréelle, plus encore qu'une photo de jeunesse: la preuve, le délit d'une pratique presque diabolique. Plus qu'un tour de passe-passe ou de prestidigitation: une machine à arrêter le temps. Car ce texte est le désespoir de l'image, et pire qu'une image floue ou voilée: une image fantôme. (*L'Image* 18)

It is important to note that throughout Guibert's work, the spectral image is nothing but a pure simulacrum, a mediator that enables the subject to disappear in order to bring death more clearly into focus. In this sense, it resembles the Blanchotian "cadaverous presence," which, like the image, "establishes a relation between here and nowhere" (*Space* 256). Even though it appropriates some elements of reality, such as family photo albums or the narrator's own photograph, it displays an infinite interplay between the real and the fake and their relation to the simulacrum. In *L'Image fantôme*, the narrator as subject is effaced in a text that supposedly draws from real life; his own photo is censored, thus making it impossible to tell whether it is he or not:

> Et soudain ce fut comme un choc, je ne pouvais pas me tromper: malignement, le garçon venait d'extraire du sac en plastique noir une photographie encore molle et l'avait aussitôt plaquée sur le verre, et sur cette photo c'était moi. Je reconnaissais mes cheveux bouclés, ma chemise blanche, ma bouche, et en même temps j'avais toute une partie du visage barrée par un appareil de rhinoscopie, ou un écouteur de radio posé à l'envers. Je n'étais jamais allé dans cette soirée, je n'avais jamais vu ce garçon. Je savais très bien que ce visage ne pouvait être que le mien (ou celui d'un sosie?), et qu'en même temps ce ne pouvait être moi. (*L'Image* 59)

The spectral image bears no relation to any *concrete* reality, as the narrator's "fictionalized" photo demonstrates. It is a body/text created in response to the "désespoir de l'image." This "despair," however, should not be understood strictly as a condemnation of photography or of images themselves;[26] rather it signifies the extent to which images, in consumer culture, are packaged "as solutions to social dilemmas, vehicles of self-identity, means to self-fulfillment" (Traube 569). Hence all the frustrated attempts throughout Guibert's work to photograph or film a particular moment only to find that the camera was never loaded to begin with, or that something, as in the above example, was blocking the object from the camera's view. Experience, as Guibert's work suggests, can never be replaced or even validated by images, which is why, as readers of his texts, we enter from the very beginning into the domain of the hyperreal and the simulacrum.

Here it is necessary to explain the role that AIDS plays in this process of simulacrum in Guibert's writing. Rather than being explored as a real phenomenon with real effects, AIDS is used more as a medium of representation. The narrator, using the destroyed body-with-AIDS, employs the elements of pain and decomposition to accentuate the (unreal) proportions of the body (he emphasizes certain body parts—like an infected lymph node in his neck or his swollen feet—as if they were being seen in a close-up by a zoom lens); this in turn allows him to re-envision and re-compose the body in hyperreal dimensions.[27]

The hyperreal body (or "cadaverous presence"), as we shall see, is constructed by/from the text through an image that acts as a body double; thus it has no relation to any real person with AIDS. Such is the case with *Mon Valet et moi* and *L'Homme au chapeau rouge,* in which we are introduced to the body-with-AIDS by means of an image. In *L'Homme au chapeau rouge,* a video image of the narrator's dying body on the operating table serves as one of the pre-texts for the narrative itself. In *Mon Valet et moi,* we are presented with an 80-year-old narrator dying of a terminal illness through the intermediary of the valet, to whom he is introduced by a photo: "A Christine, qui m'a découpé dans un magazine la photo de mon personnage, dans l'avion entre Anchorage et Tokyo, et à qui je crains que cette histoire ne dise rien du tout" (7). The problematic position of the narrator in both texts further complicates the issue, since he would seem to be telling a "true" story about his life. The narrator of *Mon Valet et moi* is a person infected with a fatal disease (possibly an element of autofiction since this story was published after Guibert's AIDS narratives). Yet the disease, albeit described in a very realistic manner, is never named and is easily attributed to old age; the narrator is supposedly 80 years old:

> J'étais un homme sur le déclin. J'avais besoin d'un vrai garde du corps, quelqu'un qui me ramasse quand je tombe, m'habille, pince mes jambes quand elles s'engourdissent au point que je ne les sens plus. (12)

> Mon valet se lève…pour me regarder dormir, et voir si tout va bien, vérifier que ma respiration est régulière…. Il n'en parle jamais, mais j'ai compris qu'il a terriblement peur que je ne meure pendant la nuit au cours de mon sommeil, c'est pourtant ce qui pourrait m'arriver de mieux…. Il faut bien qu'un homme de quatre-vingts ans parte un jour. (37)

The narrator's age, however, is consistently put into question throughout the novel: "Monsieur, c'est vrai que pour votre âge, si vous avez vraiment celui que vous prétendez, vous faites hyperjeune" (19). Thus the veracity of the narrator's discourse is immediately subverted and cannot be considered reliable/realistic information, especially since we are in the year 2036 at the end of the novel.

The Spectral Image and *Mon Valet et moi*

In *Mon Valet et moi*, the spectral image is created from the fusion of the image (a fake body double) with the body-with-AIDS. The valet functions as the body double and is nothing more than an image who appears throughout various modes of representation (e.g. cinema, literature, photography and intertextuality). First, in the dedication, as we have seen, he appears in a photo. Then, in an allusion to Russian paraliterature, he appears as a fictional character:

> Les narrateurs des romans russes ont des valets qui dorment comme des chiens dans des vestibules traversés de courants d'air, aiguisent le fleuret de leurs duels et portent leurs vieux pardessus. Ce sont des ratés, souvent des doubles de leurs maîtres, qui auraient pu l'être à leur place. (*Mon Valet* 12)

Finally, as an actor, he is said to have come to the narrator via the intermediary of cinema (thus establishing an intertext with the master of artifice, Jean Genet, who, in the following example, becomes the valet or the narrator's double): "J'aurais dû avoir l'idée le premier: aller recruter mon valet à Mettray, et l'embaucher directement sans l'intermédiaire du cinéma, qui l'a sali, dit-il, et lui a appris à mentir" (*Mon Valet* 43).

The narrator decides to hire the valet because, as we saw above, he needs a "vrai garde du corps." Significantly, throughout the novel, the valet begins to function as a double of the narrator. The narrator, disabled as a result of his disease, can no longer accomplish most everyday tasks, and needs the valet to help him regain the bodily integrity he loses in the wake of his illness. Therefore, he constructs the image of the ideal valet or the body double. This representation of the double is further complicated by the Rabelaisian manner in which the narrator introduces him:

> Au départ j'avais pensé embaucher, puisque ni mon secrétaire ni mon majordome ne pouvaient endosser *ce rôle*, et parce que je pétais de plus en plus fort dans ces soirées mondaines où je n'allais presque plus, un jeune homme élégant *qui me suivrait pas à pas* en public, mais *ferait semblant de ne pas me connaître, comme un comparse de prestidigitateur,* et s'exercerait à rougir, à toussoter et à s'excuser discrètement *à ma place* chaque fois que je lâcherais un de ces vents pétaradants. *J'imaginais,* quand j'emmènerais ce jeune homme au restaurant pour me tenir compagnie après son travail, que *par un accord tacite nous serions convenus qu'il répondrait systématiquement* au maître d'hôtel qu'il n'avait aucunement faim, et que moi je broutillerais du bout des lèvres, comme pour ne pas m'y brûler, le nappage d'un plat très copieux, que je pousserais alors sur la table en direction de mon employé, qui le dévorerait goulûment. Malheureusement, rien ne s'est passé comme prévu. (*Mon Valet* 10, my emphasis)

The valet is an image meant to respond to and simulate the narrator's fictive reality. However, things don't work out exactly as planned because when the valet takes on his role of double, he surpasses the state of imitation and obedience originally imagined by the narrator. Much like the image in Baudrillard's sense (which only conforms to the real in order to better deform it), the valet begins to contaminate and modulate the narrator's life. First, the valet assumes all the tasks of daily life once carried out by the narrator: "Maintenant c'est mon valet qui gère l'ensemble de mes affaires" (28). Then, little by little, the valet takes control of the situation:

"Mon valet…a dissimulé ou jeté presque tous mes livres préférés, que j'aimais tant relire, parce qu'il prétend qu'ils me donnent le cafard" (40). Finally, the valet deviates from his initial function so completely that he begins to abuse the narrator physically: "Il ne me parle plus, et ne répond plus à mes questions, sauf par des coups de pied" (83). At the end of the novel, the valet has returned to his obedient function, yet the narrator pushes him to begin the series of mutations again by pretending not to know him and by giving him a new identity:

> Je maugrée, pour le contrarier: 'Non, aucun souvenir. Qui es-tu? Je ne t'ai jamais vu par ici. Tu appartiens au corps des sapeurs-pompiers, c'est ça? Vous faites de la réanimation? Mais qui t'a ouvert la porte?—C'est moi, Monsieur, c'est Jim, votre valet.—Kim? C'est toi que j'ai trouvé en Thaïlande?' Je fais exprès de ne pas le reconnaître pour le pousser à bout. Quand il est à bout, il devient enfin intéressant. Il perd son exaspérante banalité. (*Mon Valet* 90)

What we are witnessing here is a constant interplay of images in a mirror or, in other words, a viral proliferation of images.[28] The valet himself is an image created from an image (the photo through which he is presented in the dedication). This proliferation of images, however, leads to an erasure of the writing subject. From one point of view, the image of the valet's body recomposes the body of the narrator—and decomposes it—by means of mass culture clothing (Nikes, Ray-Bans, baseball cap, and tight jeans). This costume is homogenous since it borrows from normative cultural stereotypes; it is also hyperreal since it mixes the real and the fake. The narrator's body, hidden behind a panoply of advertised clothing accessories, is no longer visible.[29] Because it is no more than a mixture of styles and clichés, the body facilitates the shedding of the narrator's subjectivity, even while, paradoxically, it enables the subject's very existence (as a spectral image). The more the body-with-AIDS deteriorates from its illness, the more it depends on the proliferation of images that serve as body doubles. In other words, the spectral image cannot exist without the mediation of fake body doubles. These images allow the writing subject to rehearse his death through the simulation of his existence as a series of images.[30] The status of the narrator, therefore, is always problematic since it depends on fake images (the simulacrum) to produce the text. Eventually, the narrator splits into two fictional characters: his valet and himself.

The Disappearing Portrait of the Man in the Red Hat

In *L'Homme au chapeau rouge*, the treatment of autofiction adds a new dimension to the problematizing of the real and the fake. Although the reader could think that Guibert's text is more or less autobiographical, since he writes about his own illness and his own death, the descriptions of his body as well as those of objects (especially paintings) are always positioned outside reality. In the case of the infant's portrait, the windowpane is a central element that serves as a screen between the original model (the child) and the represented object. It is a "portrait terreux—illisible" that bears the mark of a dead body:

> Le tout petit portrait d'enfant posé par terre et entraperçu derrière la vitre, brumeux, terreux, presque illisible, m'a arrêté. La plupart des tableaux que j'ai finalement achetés et dont la possession n'a plus cessé de me donner du plaisir, je les ai découverts de très loin, derrière des jeux de vitre, et dans un mouvement qui m'empêchait d'arrêter mon regard sur eux pour bien les comprendre, j'étais assis dans l'autobus, je regardais la rue par la vitre, et soudain j'apercevais dans l'arrière fond obscur d'une librairie inconnue de la rue des Martyrs ce tableau du jeune Tartitius qui est devenu mon colocataire, mon room mate depuis 1987. Le tableau conquérait de plein fouet mon désir. Je le reconnaissais comme un objet familier, une possession de toujours. (*Chapeau rouge* 25)

As the dead body or the body-with-AIDS expresses itself by a pulsion of desire, desire is directed toward a painting which, in turn, becomes a fake body double (a roommate) of the lost or dead body. However, it is precisely this meeting with an image designating death that causes the narrator to re-live. Much like Barthes's lover from the *Fragments d'un discours amoureux*, Guibert privileges the body as a "lieu d'apprentissage."[31] Looking at the paintings, it is as if he were saying "ce qui retentit en moi, c'est ce que j'apprends avec mon corps...le mot, l'image, la pensée agissent à la façon d'un coup de fouet. Mon corps intérieur se met à vibrer, comme secoué de trompettes qui se répondent et se recouvrent" (*Fragments* 237). Here, the body becomes language and then text. As Raymond Bellour has pointed out, the image in Guibert "est devenue le lieu élu d'une vacillation qui se concentre autour du corps, de la figure: elle est avant tout figuration-défiguration des corps...diluée, comme fragmentée, mais très vive et souvent d'une extrême violence, [l'image est] attachée au corps, à la pulsion, à la fois ce qui se dérobe et frappe au plus vif" ("Vérité et mensonge" 69).

The body-with-AIDS in itself is already a destroyed body. However, paradoxically, it is by means of the constant encounters with pain and destruction that the body-with-AIDS can recognize itself, and then re-compose itself. Yet, although it can re-compose itself, it is always in proportions that surpass the real:

> Ce n'était pas par masochisme, mais cette douleur me donnait une force extraordinaire, elle faisait de moi un colosse, un géant, non pas dans mon endurance à la supporter, mais parce qu'elle était devenue un instrument de connaissance de moi-même qui me grandissait dans chacune de mes pensées. (*Chapeau rouge* 41)

Guibert's newly re-constructed body takes on gigantic dimensions reminiscent of Artaud's theatrical figures, which themselves are at the origin of a new principle of writing.[32] Indeed, Guibert's descriptions of the bodies (destroyed bodies, dying bodies, shadowy bodies glimpsed through windowpanes, fragmented bodies) seen in paintings are related to writing (the space of literature in Blanchot's sense). Writing, like the body, is constantly associated with the fake (that is to say, absence). On two occasions, the narrator tells us that his manuscript has disappeared ("Le peintre partit en emportant mon texte, dont je n'avais pas le double" (43); "Ces cinquante pages égarées, qui sont maintenant Dieu sait où, j'ai beau les connaître par coeur, je suis incapable de les refaire" (154).[33] As readers, we begin to wonder where the original text is and if in fact it does exist. Moreover, the so-called real events that compose the narrative of *L'Homme au chapeau rouge* itself are another example of how writing is associated with the fake. This narrative is constantly deviating into the realm of the fake via the lie. First, as Raymond Bellour has noted, the narrator lies to the two principal characters, Yannis and Lena, by not telling them that they are in fact "les modèles" of his book. Then he lies to art brokers when he passes himself off as an American named Keith. He also lies to his best friend Jules in order to "screw" (*baiser*) him. In effect, the narrative as well as the characters are ravaged by a horror of the fake:

> En buvant du café à la cuisine, car il n'y avait rien d'autre à faire qu'à allumer le feu et regarder la télévision, nous bavardâmes un peu avec Babette. Elle m'avoua que Yannis était parti dans un état d'agitation indescriptible, ravagé, c'est le mot qu'elle employa, par cette histoire de faux. 'Pourquoi ravagé?' demandai-je 'Parce qu'il semblerait, chuchota-t-elle, que ces trente faux qu'on a retrouvés, contrairement à ce que dit Yannis en les traitant d'horreurs absolues, sont en fait de purs chefs-d'oeuvres. (*Chapeau rouge* 72)

Furthermore, the painter Yannis, suspected of having denounced his early (poorer quality) work in order to maintain his reputation and fame, becomes a double character: "Je pensai alors qu'un faux Yannis et son homme d'affaires mafioso, qui avaient peut-être mis sa ligne sur écoute et suivaient notre conversation, seraient là de toute façon…pour m'enlever et rançonner le vrai" (62). In this game of fake-real (which is also the game of writing), the reader learns quickly that she or he cannot trust anything. Hervé Guibert, as Bellour notes, "trompe enfin ses lecteurs en ne leur avouant jamais comment et jusqu'à quel degré ils sont manipulés, dans ce balancement poreux entre vie et fiction, qui confère à l'invention les apparences de la vérité autobiographique et documentaire" (69).

In effect, it is by means of the documentary and/or quasi-photographic gaze that Guibert's writing functions (in the sense of interchangeability) as an image. The image precedes the real by reversing its logical succession, that is from the real to its reproduction. Guibert's fiction, like an image, precedes the event it describes. According to Bellour, the real "serait presque avant que l'événement ne se produise, son double, son halo, sa prémonition: la phrase déjà prête à s'en emparer et à la métamorphoser" (54). The video Guibert takes of his own operation and its transformation into fiction is a good example of the real and its double, the hyperreal. The body-image here becomes more real than the real. Moreover, it is only by means of this fake-real that the text advances and exists:

Après avoir raccroché, je m'obstinai à vouloir obtenir l'image. D'un seul coup elle était là sur l'écran, bleue, métallique, à la fois chaude et glacée, irréelle, insensément belle.... Mais l'image s'était censurée d'elle-même à cause de la violente douche de lumière sur le champ opératoire, qui transformait la zone saignante et la boucherie en une zone abstraite, incandescente, comme un torrent de lumière qui jetait des rayons au niveau du cou. Avec tout un système de caches improvisé par les blouses des infirmiers qui s'interposaient entre l'angle voyeur et ce qu'on avait envie de regarder ou de ne pas voir une fois pour toutes, l'opération dissimulée de surcroît par le chirurgien et son assistante qui ressemblaient maintenant à des Martiens cannibales penchés sur leur festin, l'image était devenue d'elle-même hitchcockienne, à mort.... Quand j'arrêtai la bande, ma douleur avait redoublé, et je me mis à écrire quelque chose de tout à fait inattendu. (*Chapeau rouge* 42–43)

Alongside numerous references to the image, Guibert's writing functions much like a camera: the spectral image, floating between two extremities, is momentarily frozen in what Guibert calls "des postures de récit" (62). In this way, it exemplifies Barthes' description of photography, insofar as photography constructs and deconstructs a body according to its own "caprice:" "Photography represents that very subtle moment when, to tell the truth, I am neither subject nor object but a subject who feels he is becoming an object: I then experience a micro-version of death (of parenthesis): I am truly becoming a specter" (14).

It comes as no surprise when, at the end of the novel, we realize there is no subject behind "l'homme au chapeau rouge:" the narrator—alternately depicted as "le grand homme trop maigre au chapeau rouge" (30); "le squelette avec son chapeau rouge" (120); "une silhouette noire surmontée d'une tache rouge" (150)—is ultimately nothing more than a fractal image, a self-effacing spectral image of death.[34]

Photographic writing and the body-with-AIDS permit Hervé Guibert to suspend time—immobilize it—so as to modulate it, not only in order to control the fear of death, but also to bring his readers into a face-to-face confrontation with it. The figure of death—the spectral image—is always present; it is the leitmotif that haunts the text. What is remarkable about Guibert is that the production of texts ends up replacing the dead body according to a principle of fractal representation. This new body-of-writing, composed of objects, fetishes, images, paintings, photos and videos, becomes more real than the real; it is the primitive theater of death. [35]

~~~~~~

Anthony Giddens has commented on the fact that "…we don't really have morally viable ways of handling sickness, death, existential crises of life" today, "because they're undercut by the very nature of the world we live in, which is based on the idea of technology and control…" (qtd. in Tomlinson 113). Certainly, images have been put to use in late-modern globalization to strengthen our ties to technological mastery over death, suffering, and disease, a function recognized and described by Guibert as

> commune, et presque vulgaire…car n'est-ce pas le lot de tous les reporters, de tous les photographes envoyés sur les guerres, les catastrophes ou les famines, de rapporter la photo la plus près possible de la mort, et même parfois la photo de la mort?…. Une photo qui représente la mort, l'instant qui la précède tout juste, ou qui la suit, tout juste encore, et toujours au plus près, dans le temps ou dans l'espace, même si elle est mauvaise techniquement, floue, ou mal cadrée, même si le photographe est un inconnu, est déjà en soi une photo commercialisable: à coup sûr elle trouvera des médias, et des satellites, pour la passer et la diffuser d'un pays à l'autre. Elle sera reproduite, et multipliée à l'infini; *elle restera dans les imaginations, innombrable et suspendue, toujours vibrante, comme une petite menace, ou la délectation d'être soi hors du cadre, et de voir encore.* (L'Image 150, my emphasis)

In his evocation of the viewers of such images as sadistic voyeurs, casual thrill-seekers, Guibert points to the "necrophiliac perversion" of our image culture in its screening of blood, violence and death. The screen here encourages a morbid voyeurism, as the spectator-self takes pleasure in its ability to survive the death of the Other and therefore to symbolically conquer death itself. As Robins explains, this detached screen-gazing renders embodied (moral) engagement with the real world more difficult since "the screen bypasses the intractable nature of reality, and it seems to put us in control of the world" (80).

By turning the image into a dead body, a Blanchotian "cadaverous presence" or spectral image, Hervé Guibert returns it, as Barthes would say, to a "primitive" context in which it maintains a symbolic (reciprocal) relationship with death. Indeed, through the literal *incorporation* of the photographic image into his own body, as the below example from *L'Image fantôme* demonstrates, Guibert is able to "deliver" the image from its "sickness," that is to say its association with rationality, technical mastery, and fixed identity. In the following passage, entitled "L'image cancéreuse," the narrator has been living in a state of fascination with the image of an unknown boy for seven years. One day, he notices that the image has started a gradual process of decomposition upon which he declares the image "cancerous." Trying to find a way to "bury" the boy's image, the narrator, finding no other method to destroy it acceptable, veils it, but this does not stop it from haunting him. Next, he undertakes a process of transubstantiation when he places the image in his bed,

> sous le drap qui accueillait mon corps, je l'écrasais et je l'entendais geindre. Il vivait dans mes rêves. Je le cousais dans mon oreiller. Puis, quelque temps, je me décidai à le porter directement sur moi, à même ma peau, à même mon torse, en l'y attachant avec des bandes et des élastiques…. Il était comme un second frère mort attaché à moi, il était mon hétéradelphe. Quand je me décidai enfin à m'en détacher…je m'aperçus que le carton ramolli était vide, l'image était blanche, mais elle ne s'était pas évaporée…. Dans une glace, je vérifiais qu'elle avait adhéré à ma peau, comme un tatouage ou une décalcomanie. Chaque pigment chimique du papier avait trouvé sa place dans un des pores de ma peau. Et la même image se recomposait exactement, à l'envers. Le transfert l'avait délivré de sa maladie… (*L'Image* 169)

The image for Guibert, in its ability to sollicit and fascinate the subject, breaks down the usual distinctions between the living and the dead to create a subject that is always already fractured (fractal). This split subject, like the "primitive" and his double, embodies the living figure of the dead.[36]

NOTES

1. Guibert writes about Foucault in two works: "Les secrets d'un homme," part of the collection of short stories entitled *Mauve le Vierge*, and *A l'ami qui ne m'a pas sauvé la vie*. While many critics mention the fact that Guibert writes Foucault into his so-called confessional narratives, I refer the reader here to Raymond Bellour's discussion of this topic in his article "Une entreprise qui n'eut jamais d'exemple...," since I feel he captures the experimentation behind Guibert's project, as well as Foucault's knowing participation in it. See especially pp. 122–123.

2. Guibert has written many famous people and friends—such as Isabelle Adjani, Balthus, Bacon, Duras, Barthes and others—into his books.

3. Brian McHale describes the process of "throwing a fictional party for one's real-life friends" as a typical case of "transworld identity between real and fictional identities. This is a particularly heightened form of ontological boundary-violation" (203) found in postmodernist autobiography.

4. For a pertinent discussion of the rise of exhibitionism see, to give only one example, "Media Knowledges, Warrior Citzenry, and Postmodern Literacies," by Peter McLaren and Rhonda Hammer, especially pp. 102–103 and 110–111.

5. As James Kirkup's comments from an obituary published less than a month after Guibert's death on December 27, 1991, testify. Kirkup's description of Guibert—true to Bellour's predictions—shuns all critical distance in favor of a scandalous tone more befitting a television talk show host than a literary critic:

   > Guibert made no secret of his sexual orientation in his work and in his life. He detested hypocrisy, humbug and censorship in all its forms, and candidly laid himself open to scandalous attacks from *bien pensants* who accused him of paedophilia and proclaimed him mad and perverted. The world of gay bars, saunas and hard-core homo movies in which he lived is well recorded.... But this was not his only world, for he was an aesthete, an artist and a perfectionist in photography. A dedicated narcissist, in love with his own angelic beauty, he took many revealing photographs of himself and his boyfriends. (25)

As Murray Pratt notes, "Cette réception est en elle-même indicative du degré selon lequel ceux qui parlent de leur homosexualité sont toujours pris en spectacle" (75).

6. For discussions of the pathologization of society and media consumption, see "Media Knowledges, Warrior Citzenry, and Postmodern Literacies," by Peter McLaren and Rhonda Hammer as well as *Into the Image* by Kevin Robins.

7. Paul Rambali describes the cultural context in which *La Pudeur et l'impudeur* (a home-movie filmed by Guibert that charts his deterioration in the face of AIDS), and Guibert's two AIDS narratives *A l'ami qui ne m'a pas sauvé la vie* and *Le Protocole compassionnel*, were received: "In the theatrical milieu of Paris... homosexuality is not made public, not even as camp. Guibert had been one of the few French artists to reveal that he was HIV-positive. He made of it neither the pop condomania of Keith Haring, nor the campaigning fervour of Derek Jarman, but an agitated personal confessional...in which his frankness edged on scandal. For many, including many French homosexuals who didn't appreciate his indiscretion, Guibert's book and its sequel...were the work of a childish provocateur who wanted the whole world to hear his dernier cri" (22).

8. Foucault has described Guibert's work as belonging to "...ces formes de travail qui ne s'avancent pas comme une oeuvre, mais qui s'ouvrent parce qu'elles sont des expériences" (qtd. in Bellour 122).

9. As Jean-Pierre Boulé writes, "Hervé Guibert a toujours eu le projet de tout écrire. On voit bien que ce souhait s'inscrit en filigrane de la totalité de son oeuvre" ("Introduction" 2). I will return to this element of Guibert's aesthetic below.

10. Some examples, widely publicized by the news media and prime time television, include videotapings of police brutality in Los Angeles, abuses inflicted on the elderly in managed care facilities, and babysitters mistreating children under the watchful eye of the camera in parents' homes. The actualization of experience through filming finds perhaps its most extreme fulfillment in cases where people videotape themselves in criminal acts such as arson, sex crimes, and even murder.

11. See Pierre Sorlin's *Mass Media*, chapter two, for a discussion of media as instruments of sociability.

12. Susan Bordo articulates this tension through an analysis of consumer culture: "With created images setting the standard, we are becoming habituated to the glossy and gleaming, the smooth and shining, the ageless and sagless and

wrinkleless. We are learning to expect 'perfection' and to find any 'defect' repellent, unacceptable. We expect live performances to sound like CDs, politicians to say nothing messy or disturbing, real breasts to be as round and firm as implants" (*Twilight Zones* 3).

13. Edward Said articulates this problematic in the context of multiculturalism and political correctness in his penultimate Reith Lecture, "Speaking Truth to Power," which concerns the position of intellectuals today. As he states,

> not only did a consensus disappear on what constituted objective reality, but a lot of traditional authorities, including God, were in the main swept away.... The critique of objectivity and authority did perform a positive service by underlining how, in the secular world, human beings construct their truths, so to speak.... [Yet] now everyone comes forward with new and often violently opposed views of the world.... There is now more intolerance and strident assertiveness abroad everywhere than any one system can handle. The result is an almost complete absence of universals, even though very often the rhetoric suggests, for instance, that 'our' values (whatever these may happen to be) are in fact universal. (12)

14. Jean-Pierre Boulé addresses the interactive element in Guibert's work in his discussion of the author's direct or indirect interpellations of the reader. See "Hervé Guibert à la télévision: vérité et séduction," pp. 119–120.

15. For a discussion of the ways in which image and vision technologies screen out reality and experience of the real world in favor of a contained (and therefore safe) environment, see Kevin Robins's *Into the Image*, especially chapters one and six.

16. Several critics have pointed out the intertext with Barthes's work established throughout Guibert's texts. See, for example, Edmund Smyth's "Des Aveugles: Modes D'Articulation" and Murray Pratt's "De la Désidentification à l'Incognito: A la recherche d'une autobiographique homosexuelle."

17. The "ontological flicker" (a term borrowed here from Brian McHale) provoked by the image operates similarly in postmodern auto-bio-graphy: in both cases, there is a vacillation between presence and absence, a subject and a decentered subject. In postmodernist literature, like Guibert's, "the author flickers in and out of existence at different levels of the ontological structure and at different points in the unfolding text" (McHale 202).

18. From this perspective, postmodern writer Ronald Sukenick's comments concerning the use of self in the postmodern novel apply to Guibert: "We were not writing autobiography or confession—we were at times using those forms as ways of incorporating our experience into fiction at the same level as any other data" (qtd. in McHale 203).

19. Marie Darrieussecq, for example, reads *L'Incognito* from the perspective of AIDS, even though it was published before it was known that Guibert had AIDS, as she notes in her disclaimer: "Toutefois il faut rappeler que la lecture que nous faisons là de *L'Incognito* est une lecture *a posteriori*, après les romans du sida, et après la mort de Guibert. En 1989, ce livre déconcertant pouvait véritablement être lu comme une énigme, au niveau du roman policier, et au niveau, aussi, de son sens général" (87). See "La Notion de leurre chez Hervé Guibert."

20. Derek Duncan makes a similar point in the context of gay subjectivity and political activism: "Les dernières oeuvres de Guibert sont traversées par la connaissance de sa séropositivité mais, pour Guibert, la conscience qu'il est atteint du sida fera partie d'un projet artistique et autobiographique déjà entamé plutôt que d'un activisme politique à découvrir" (101).

21. This premise is illustrated throughout Guibert's texts where he describes medical procedures through filmic references (e.g. Hitchcock films or films about the Holocaust such as *Nuit et brouillard*) or, as in *Protocole compassionnel*, other PWA's through horror film terminology: "Vraiment de jeunes cadavres aux yeux de braise, comme sur des affices de films d'horreur où des morts ressortent de leurs tombes et font quelques pas en vacillant" (46). Derek Duncan interprets the fact that Guibert refers to a film about the Holocaust instead of to the direct historical reality as proof that the use of this image is more aesthetic than political. I would argue that given the contemporary context, in which the historical referent has been problematized alongside reality itself, Guibert's reference to film strikes a cord with reader/viewer experience. It is therefore political insofar as it speaks to the contemporary environment in which History, as well as the experience of death, stages itself.

22. In saying this, I do not intend by any means to discount the importance of Guibert's writing on AIDS and its significance in giving voice to the homophobia (medical and otherwise) and racism that has ruled much of the discourse surrounding the epidemic. Since it is my intention to underline the links between subjective experience and the image in Guibert, my focus necessarily incorporates AIDS as a medium functioning similarly to the image, a correlation that has been drawn out by cultural critics of the information age. For pertinent discussions of the political and emotional impact of Guibert's

AIDS narratives, see David Caron's "Playing Doctors: Refiguring the Doctor-Patient Relationship in Hervé Guibert's AIDS Novels," Lawrence R. Schehr's "Hervé Guibert under Bureaucratic Quarantine," and Emily Apter's "Fantom Images: Hervé Guibert and the Writing of sida in France."

23. AIDS, "the first major illness known by an acronym" (Sontag, *AIDS and its Metaphors* 28), is a virtual disease not only because of its undefinable nature, but also because it is part of a cultural landscape that technologizes experience to the point where it becomes an object of consumption, unreal in its effects. "Random Access Memory, Acquired Immune Deficiency Syndrome, Mutual Assured Destruction" (Robins 126).

24. Susan Sontag tells us that in accounts of AIDS, infection is described like high-tech warfare. She cites the following account from *Time* magazine: "'On the surface of that cell, it finds a receptor into which one of its envelope proteins fits perfectly, like a key into a lock. Docking with the cell, the virus penetrates the cell membrane and is stripped of its protective shell in the process...' Next the invader takes up permanent residence, by a form of alien takeover familiar in science-fiction narratives. The body's own cells *become* the invader. With the help of an enzyme the virus carries with it 'the naked AIDS virus converts its RNA into...DNA, the master molecule of life. The molecule then penetrates the cell nucleus, inserts itself into a chromosome and takes over part of the cellular machinery, directing it to produce more AIDS viruses. Eventually, overcome by its alien product, the cell swells and dies, releasing a flood of new viruses to attack other cells...'" (*AIDS and Its Metaphors* 18).

25. See Baudelaire's cult of images in *Mon coeur mis à nu*.

26. For a more detailed analysis of the intersections between photography and writing in Guibert, see Alain Buisine.

27. Steven Shaviro's remarks on David Cronenberg's films apply to Guibert's use of image technologies to probe the body: "Video technology is no longer concerned merely with disembodied images. It reaches directly into the unseen depths, stimulating the ganglia and the viscera, caressing and remolding the interior volume of the body" (142).

28. This becomes even more striking when the narrator says: "Quand nous sortons ensemble dans les rues de Bangkok, mon valet et moi, une fois que le déluge a cessé, j'ai l'illusion de nous voir en permanence dans un

grand miroir qu'un esclave porterait sur son dos en sautillant devant nous. Je nous distingue lui et moi, avec nos habillements semblables, et parfois, je n'arrive plus à savoir si c'est lui à gauche, ou moi à droite, comme si nous étions une seule personne dédoublée. Parfois aussi je nous surprends dans le miroir transformés en femmes...je porte des lunettes noires panoramiques entièrement opaques, je sais que j'ai quatre-vingts ans, mais de loin j'ai l'air d'en avoir dix-huit, cette vision n'a pas fini de m'enchanter" (60).

29. The narrator, in reference to his valet and his clothing, says "J'ai toujours été habile à tromper mon monde. Mon valet et moi, nous passons quasi inaperçus. Nous avons l'air de deux jeunes comme les autres, de deux frères. J'ai quatre-vingts ans mais en voyage je porte des chaussures de tennis Nike rembourrées, des jeans serrés, des blousons de cuir, mes Ray Ban cachent mes pattes-d'oie et ma casquette les raccords de bistouri des liftings.... J'ai l'impression de vivre une nouvelle jeunesse" (15).

30. Guibert's use of simulacra to rehearse death is a typical feature of postmodernist fiction. As Brian McHale explains, "Postmodernist writing models or simulates death; it produces simulacra of death through confrontations between worlds, through transgressions of ontological levels or boundaries, or through vacillation between different kinds and degrees of 'reality'" (232).

31. Barthes tells us that the lover is not to be reduced to a "symptomal subject," but rather that we understand him/her as "the body's gesture caught in action and not contemplated in repose...what in the straining body can be immobilized" (*A Lover's Discourse* 4)

32. For a discussion of Artaud's theatrical figures and writing, see Dominique Fisher's "L'Abstrait et le concret d'Artaud."

33. This also occurs in *Mon Valet et moi*. For example, "Je dicte mon livre à mon valet, il prend en note docilement tout ce que je lui ordonne d'écrire, et ne fait aucun commentaire, ensuite je relis pour vérifier s'il n'a rien censuré" (86).

34. For a pertinent discussion on how the death of the subject comes to bear on the conjunction of AIDS and postmodernism, see Lee Edelman's "The Mirror and the Tank: 'AIDS,' Subjectivity, and the Rhetoric of Activism" in *Writing AIDS*, pp. 9–37.

35. I am referring to Barthes's *Tableau Vivant*: "However 'lifelike' we strive to make it (and this frenzy to be lifelike can only be our mythic denial of an apprehension of death), Photography is a kind of primitive theater, a kind of *Tableau Vivant*, a figuration of the motionless and made-up face beneath which we see the dead" (*Camera Lucida* 31–32). The same could be said of Guibert's writing.

36. As Baudrillard explains, "[t]he double, like the dead man (the dead man is the double of the living, the double is the familiar living figure of the dead), is a *partner* with whom the primitive has a personal and concrete relationship, sometimes happy, sometimes not, a certain type of visible exchange (word, gesture and ritual) with an invisible part of himself" (*Symbolic Exchange and Death* 141). Guibert's descriptions of paintings in *L'Homme au chapeau rouge* as roommates; the various tableaux in *L'Image fantôme* in which the image takes on qualities of living beings (e.g. "La Preuve par l'absurde," pp. 157–160); and the elements of superstition and the occult throughout his work can be connected, in my view, to this phenomenon.

4 | Bouraoui's Ghosts: Projections of Women in the Nineties

...les Mauresques plaintives se renvoient le murmure du semblable, l'hymne à la douleur commune, il faut être attentive et vigilante afin de l'attraper au vol avant qu'il ne s'écrase sur la chaussée séparatrice.

—*Nina Bouraoui*

For the master's tools will never dismantle the master's house...

—*Audre Lorde*

In 1991, Nina Bouraoui captured the attention of the French literary world with the publication of her first novel, *La Voyeuse interdite*, a tale narrated in the first person which graphically depicts the psychic and physical mutilations undergone by a young sequestered woman living in Algeria. Praised by critics for her incisive and tightly woven prose, rich in word-play and symbolic imagery similar to that of Rimbaud or Breton,[1] Bouraoui was awarded the *Prix du Livre Inter* in 1991 and has since published five novels—*Poing mort* (1992), *Le Bal des murènes* (1996), *L'Age blessé* (1998), *Le Jour du séisme* (1999), and *Garcon manqué* (2000). In several of her intensely poetic novels, Bouraoui represents extremely violent parent-child relationships, focusing specifically on the image of a cruel and murderous mother capable of spawning only death and destruction. Significantly, the struggle between mother and child in Bouraoui's texts manifests itself in and through the (female or feminized) body, whence the presence of (self)mutilation, putrefaction, anorexia, defiguration, and disease throughout her work.

Bouraoui's representation of the female gendered body, in its obsessive detail to bodily functions and sensual experiences, would appear to be in sharp contrast with the increasing dematerialization of the body in technoculture. After all, as we have been discussing throughout our analysis, "contemporary culture, technologically armed, seems bent on defying aging, our various biological 'clocks,' and even death itself" (Bordo, *Unbearable Weight* 5). However, as I will address in this chapter, Bouraoui's aesthetic articulates technoculture's attempt to transcend corporeal reality through the representation of the female subject locked in battle with her body, a scenario that echoes contemporary forms of female empowerment fostered by the media, and which is exemplified strikingly in Bouraoui via the figure of the anorectic. Indeed, it could even be said that Bouraoui's texts allegorically embody, through female figures, precisely those elements of culture that are disavowed in the space of the screen, namely contact with the Other's body and, subsequently, with death.

In *La Voyeuse interdite*, the text to be discussed in this chapter, culture's disavowal of bodily contact with the Other appears through the stories told by a young female narrator, Fikria, who has been isolated in her room since the onset of menstruation (significantly, she also remains nameless until the last pages of the novel). Deprived of contact with the outside world due to her newly acquired status as an *impure* sexual object, she situates herself in front of her window and, like Scheherazade before her, composes stories "dans la chambre des mille et une peines" (139) as if her life depended on it. The window, presented by the narrator as a place fraught with danger, mystery, and freedom, thus provides the young woman with an outlet onto the world (she may see it and describe it) even as it blocks her access to it (she may not effect change within it). In this sense, the narrator's window models the screen of the television or the cinema for "it symbolizes how we now exist in the world, our contradictory condition of engagement and disengagement" (Robins 77). In other words, in front of her window, Fikria is not an actor but rather a spectator.

This distinction between actor and spectator is an important one for whereas both positions interpellate the social agent, they imply different levels of control over the cultural practices that produce social relations in image culture. To a large degree, as Robins suggests, the split between actor and spectator enacted through the screen has become a collective experience. Using the screening of the Gulf War as an example, he refers to a splitting mechanism prevalent in culture today whereby "[t]he spectator-self is morally disengaged, floating about in an ocean of violent images. The actor-self is caught up in a reality whose violence is often morally overwhelming.... [T]he spectator and the actor seem to be going their separate ways" (81).

Where female spectatorship is concerned, however, the distinction between the actor-self and the spectator-self requires additional qualification, for the very act of a woman looking in patriarchal[2] culture (as the title *La Voyeuse interdite* precisely indicates) evokes the more fundamental split between masculinity and femininity, subject and object—notions which themselves are constructed around a specific (masculinist) perception and representation of space. As John Berger aptly describes,

> To be born a woman has been to be born, within an allotted and confined space, into the keeping of men. The social presence of women has developed as a result of their ingenuity in living under such tutelage within such a limited space. But this has been at the cost of a woman's self being split into two. A woman must continually watch herself. *She is almost continually accompanied by her own image of herself.... And so she comes to consider the surveyor and the surveyed within her as the two constituent yet always distinct elements of her identity as a woman.* (*Ways of Seeing* 46, my emphasis)

Where men's class, social, and economic power is aligned with the power (subject) of the gaze—which itself is presented since modernity as a tool by which to master and control the object of vision—woman, as object of the gaze, necessarily figures as Other, even to (within) herself.[3] Femininity is thus produced in opposition to masculinity, that is to say as an object of visibility which is performed through gestures, voice, clothes and other theatrical devices such as make-up and masquerade. John Berger formulated the following statement as a means to articulate this tension:

> [M]*en act* and *women appear.* Men look at women. Women watch themselves being looked at. This determines not only most relations between men and women but also the relation of women to themselves. The surveyor of woman in herself is male: the surveyed female. Thus she turns herself into an object—and most particularly an object of vision: a sight. (*Ways of Seeing* 47, emphasis in original)

Indeed, as Griselda Pollock has noted, the regime described here by Berger has been so powerful that the cultural construction of femininity through the artifice of beauty and representation no longer appears to us as artificial but rather as natural. In other words, from the European nude to advertising images today, women have been positioned for so long as beautiful objects of consumption for the male gaze that "[t]he ideological construction of an absolute category woman has been effaced and this regime of representation has naturalized woman as image, beautiful to look at, defined by her 'looks'" (Pollock 121).

In *La Voyeuse interdite*, the evacuation of real women and their transformation into vacuous images is raised by the representation of the veil and the division of space into the separate spheres of public (visible) and private (hidden), a division that is enacted, moreover, in both Western and non-Western contexts. Defining a woman by her "looks," then, does not necessarily translate into *showing* a woman's body; it can also amount to *hiding* it. In the following example, in which Fikria gazes at the other windows on her street that conceal young women like her, the curtain acts as a veil to simultaneously hide and reveal the women, who are therefore present only in absence, that is to say silence and death:

> Un jeu d'ombres, de lumières et de nuances habiles entre le clair et l'obscur révèle la présence des jeunes filles avides d'événements, *encadrées* par leurs fenêtres, debout, droites et sérieuses derrière la popeline des rideaux clos, elles *ornent* comme des *statues* érigées à la gloire du silence et de l'aparté les immeubles vétustes; *réduites à l'état de pierre inanimée*, prêcheuses muettes, guetteuses clandestines, vicieuses ignorantes suspendues par un fil divin au-dessus de la chaussée des fantasmes, elles narguent les hommes, le désir et la promiscuité. (11, my emphasis)

In turning her gaze to the windows, where young girls and women are constantly yet barely perceptible behind closed curtains, Bouraoui's narrator again conjures up the spectral projections of the space of the screen— indeed, it is only by dint of "un jeu d'ombres, de lumières et de nuances habiles entre le clair et l'obscur" (11) necessary to photographic or cinematographic representation that the women in this text may be deciphered at all:

Un oeil curieux, une bouche tordue, un bras agité donnent vie aux paquets de chair ficelés dans des voiles grisâtres; vus de ma fenêtre, les fantômes borgnes paraissent asexués mais, si on les observe avec plus d'attention, on devine, se tortillant sous le costume traditionnel, des formes trop grasses pour être masculines. Elles ricanent, jurent, injurient sous la petite vitrine béante... (18)

In her presentation of these women as mere statues, ghostly projections, or even jewels (they are "réduites à l'état de pierre inanimée" to better ornament the "windows"), the "voyeuse interdite" (as her appellation amply demonstrates) self-consciously and critically positions herself within patriarchal cultural traditions that represent woman as image, a move that has effectively silenced women by placing them as objects in the subject/object divide.[4]

This brings us to a fundamental contradiction that arises for female spectators, especially those who are women artists: How are women, who see their experience "in terms of the feminine position, that is as object of the look," to "account for the feelings [they] experience as...subject of the look" (Pollock 86)? Or in other words, how are women to transcend the subject/object, mind/body dualism instated through the scopic regime of patriarchal cultural practices in order to build other, different ways of seeing and being?

La Voyeuse interdite articulates these very questions through the perspective of a young female narrator who, as she composes stories while looking out of her bedroom window (a space to which she is confined against her will), symbolizes the position of the woman artist whose mind is free to occupy the public, masculine sphere of the city street while her body is restricted (symbolically if not literally) to the private, feminine sphere of the house:

Sans effort, j'arrive à extraire des trottoirs un geste, un regard, une situation qui me donnent plus tard la sève de l'aventure. L'imagination part de presque rien, une fenêtre, un trolley, une petite fille et son curieux sourire, puis, là, s'étale devant moi un nouveau tapis d'histoires tissé de mots et de maux que je stoppe avec un noeud grossier: le lyrisme. Je ne suis pas dupe de ma vision des choses. A mon gré, elles se travestissent, s'arrachent à la banalité du vraiment vrai, elles se réclament, s'interchangent et, une fois le masque posé sur leur étrange figure immuable, elles se donnent en spectacle. (10)

Fikria's imagination can indeed carry her away from "la banalité du vraiment vrai," that is to say the real world in which she is required to remain "tapie derrière [s]a fenêtre. Là, spectatrice clandestine suspendue au-dessus de la ville, [elle] ne risque rien" (21). This position is similar to that of contemporary screen-gazers who, isolated in their homes or offices, can experience the "world" at a safe distance in cyberspace or by tele-vision. However, because her imagination is restricted by the space of the screen—"un rectangle bien délimité par des bâtisses sombres et anguleuses" (9)—Fikria's vision is also limited. She is powerless to see beyond the spectacle that projects itself daily on the screen that is her window. The restrictions placed on her body, then, indeed interfere with her creativity and prohibit her from finding a place in the world which she herself could define. The screen in this sense thus replaces reality. "And the replacement," as John Berger has argued, "is a double one. For reality is born of the encounter of consciousness and events. To deny reality is not simply to deny what is objective. It is also to deny an essential part of the subjective" (qtd. in Robins 71). At the end of the novel, when Fikria is forced into marriage, her artistic capacity and subjectivity will have all but disappeared, leaving in their place the only creativity that is tolerated from women within the confines of the patriarchal society portrayed in this book: motherhood (I will return to this below).

If I have gone to such lengths thus far to establish an analogy between Fikria's position and the position of contemporary screen-gazers, it is because I believe that La Voyeuse interdite constitutes a space of critical reflection on the contradictory positions women occupy in transnational globalized technoculture. For while contemporary cultural practices seek to defy "the historicity, the mortality, and, indeed, the very materiality of the body" (Bordo, Unbearable Weight 245) through the use of medical and image technologies on the one hand, female bodies continue to serve as markers of tradition as well as of national and cultural identity on the other. As Avtar Brah explains, women occupy a central place in the processes of signification embedded in racism and nationalism.... [W]omen are crucial to the construction and reproduction of nationalist ideologies. Women may serve as the symbolic figuration of a nation. They are also seen as embodiments of male honour, and as such become a site of contestation for this honour.... When represented as guardians of the 'race' and nation women not only signify and demarcate juridical, political, cultural and psychic boundaries of a national collectivity but they inscribe these boundaries in and through a myriad of cultural practices. (16)[5]

La Voyeuse interdite actualizes the contradictory cultural positions women occupy today via Fikria's double performance as narrating subject and repressed bodily object. Moreover, as we will address further, Bouraoui's representation of women of different ages, classes, economic capacities, races, and religions in this text also contributes to a multi-dimensional portrait of women's lives, drawing out the "dense nature of power relations in the postcolonial [postmodern] world"[6] rather than reducing women to simple victims of an oppressive system (Bahri 3). Yet the image that most strikingly captures the complexity of women's experience in *La Voyeuse interdite* is that of the anorectic.

Previously in this chapter, we discussed the subject/object, mind/body split that lies at the basis of female spectatorship and women's subjectivity. Within this paradigm, the woman's body is the "scene of enactment" of patriarchal systems of thought (Bahri 3), serving as a privileged object over which men as subjects are defined. The female body, therefore, impedes the development of a feminine subject position. Yet we also discussed contemporary culture's attempts to transcend the body with the assistance of new medical and image technologies such as plastic surgery and cyberspace, a movement that is linked to the dematerialization of the body in the space of the screen. Within these technologically-driven scenarios, since a person's real physical appearance is replaced by the artifice of simulation, it would seem that women's dilemma with the body is easily solved. Free to alter herself to her own specifications—her body becoming a sort of cultural plastic—woman is empowered with the help of technology to exercise her agency without interference from her body. When we consider the case of the anorectic, whose mind is mobilized against her body, it becomes clear, however, that the historically ingrained ideology concerning the duality between the mind and the body still persists, despite some modulations in its manifestations. What I would like to concentrate on now, then, is the convergence of these alternate discursive spaces within the condition known as anorexia nervosa as it is represented in *La Voyeuse interdite*. Nevertheless, before taking up anorexia specifically, I must first briefly revisit the motif of the mind/body dualism in order to address its specificity in relation to women's lives in technoculture. We will see that this dualism resurfaces in contemporary media discourses addressing women's subjectivity, and it is embraced by the anorectic as a way of enabling her self-realization. This is also what is at stake for the anorectic in Bouraoui's novel. I turn now, then, to a discussion of women's subjectivity, the female body, and their figuration in contemporary discourses.

Locating the Female Body in Culture Today

Feminists have shown that throughout history, the body has been conceptualized in opposition to the mind, creating a dualism wherein "that which is not-body is the highest, the best, the noblest, the closest to God" and "that which is body is the albatross, the heavy drag on self-realization" (Bordo, *Unbearable Weight* 5). Women, assigned to the role of the body in patriarchal myths due to her powers of reproduction, as well as to male desires to control female sexuality and autonomy, thus came to represent the negative pole in a series of dualisms all too familiar to feminists today: culture/nature, Mary/Eve, active/passive, life/death. As Elisabeth Bronfen aptly summarizes,

> [u]sing the feminine form as allegory of nature, European culture could express nature as the mother and bride, whose primary life-giving functions were to comfort, nurture, and provide. Yet nature also embodied unruly disorder, uncivilised wilderness, famines and tempests that threatened generation by destroying crops and killing infants. In the equation with nature, earth, body, Woman was construed as Other to culture, as object of intense curiosity to be explored, dissected, conquered, domesticated and, if necessary, eliminated. (66) [7]

Ample scholarship has pointed to the concrete social effects of the mind/body dualism on the psychic, physical, emotional, and political experience of women. Adrienne Rich, for example, has analyzed the normalization of coercive cultural practices that seek to control the female body and place it into the hands of male-defined institutions (e.g. medicine, law, literary and artistic representations), a phenomenon she identifies as compulsive heterosexuality. The fashion and beauty industries, wherein women are construed as "their own worst enemies," are also primary sites for the institutionalization and ongoing maintenance of female submission to the body.[8] Moreover, these institutions are not free of the hegemonic discourses of Eurocentrism, such that, while all women are subjected to patriarchal mechanisms of bodily control, white women are constituted as the only legitimate objects of desire. As Ella Shohat and Robert Stam affirm,

> The hegemony of this Eurocentric gaze, spread not only by First World media but even at times by Third World media, explains why morena women in Puerto Rico, like Arab-Jewish (Sephardi) women in Isreal, dye their hair blonde, why Brazilian TV commercials are more suggestive of Scandinavia than of a Black majority country, why 'Miss Universe' contests can elect blonde 'queens' even in order to appear more Western.... The mythical norms of Eurocentric esthetics come to inhabit the intimacy of self-consciousness, leaving severe psychic wounds. A patriarchal system contrived to generate neurotic self-dissatisfaction in *all* women (whence anorexia, bulimia, and other pathologies of appearance) becomes especially oppressive for women of color by excluding them from the realms of legitimate images of desire. (322)

Inevitably, whenever one undertakes an analysis of the complex power relations at work in culture's grip on the female body, the question of women's agency and subjectivity arises. Many will object to what they perceive as the reduction of women to passive objects or "victims" within the networks of power, networks which, after all, constitute these very same objects as subjects capable in their own right not only of resistance, but also of oppression. The erasure of lesbians and women of color from much cultural and feminist scholarship has served precisely as a point of contention within theorizations of the specificity of female experience and of woman-as-body. Indeed, contemporary feminist criticism, in the wake of poststructuralism and postmodernism, has come close to abandoning the notion of gendered experience altogether, preferring instead to concentrate on the body as an open signifier and its potential to theoretically destabilize conventional interpretations of masculinity and femininity, homosexuality and heterosexuality.

The deterritorialization of the female body from gender—that is to say from its connections to "femaleness" as a stable (embodied) category by which to analyze women's social experience—has pushed feminist criticism in many directions.[9] More and more, however, as *Time* magazine's June 29, 1998 cover story "Feminism: It's all about me!" points to, contemporary feminists are turning their backs on systemic cultural critique to focus instead on what Bordo has called "power feminism." Power feminism, as Bordo brilliantly describes, blurs the lines between technocratic capitalism and certain strains of (postmodern/"postfeminist") academic discourse in its emphasis on female "agency." She writes,

> 'power feminists' are telling us that we're past all those tiresome harangues about 'the beauty system' and 'objectification' and 'starving girls.' What's so bad about makeup anyway? Isn't it my right to go for it? Do what I want with my body? Be all that I can be?.... Getting one's body in shape, of course, has become the exemplary practice, symbol, and means of empowerment in this culture. 'You don't just shape your body,' as Bally Fitness tells us. 'You shape your life'.... [The] rhetoric of taking charge of one's own life has been yoked to everything.... Among some academic feminists, an insistence on the efficacy of female 'agency' is the more moderate, sober, scholarly sister of 'power feminism.' (*Twilight Zones* 34–5)

"Agency feminists" (such as Katie Roiphe and Camille Paglia) have positioned themselves in opposition to what they cast as the "old" feminism of the sixties and seventies, a feminism which supposedly views women as "passive victims" and "helpless pawns" in the face of social forces "beyond their control."[10] Today, in contrast, "feminism respects and honors the individual's choices as a locus of personal power, creativity, [and] self-definition" over and, in many cases, *beyond* the body (Bordo, *Twilight Zones* 36). From this perspective, a whole range of cultural practices that were hitherto considered oppressive to women by feminists (e.g. date rape; beauty practices such as dieting, corseting, high heels, and surgical alterations; the veil; and even pornography) are now recast as vehicles of empowerment, opportunities for women to choose, refashion, and take control of their lives.[11]

The above discussion is not meant to discredit the valorization of experimentation with identity or experiences of contradictory subjectivities that is a staple of much postmodern criticism today. Rather, it is intended to highlight contemporary epistemological configurations at work in feminism in which the mind (agency, interpretation, subjectivity) is privileged over the body (the cultural and social effects of bodily practices), a state of affairs which is, to say the least, incredibly problematic for feminist analysis given the historical subjection of women to the body.[12] In the following section, I will bring the contemporary privileging of agency to bear on two social phenomena, anorexia nervosa and cyberspace, in order to point to some limits of disembodied forms of empowerment. From this vantage point, we will be in a better position to understand the mechanisms at work in *La Voyeuse interdite*, in which Fikria and her sister Zohr target their bodies as sites on which to launch an attack against a corrupt social structure. In their attempts to "rewrite" the female body through self-starvation and self-mutilation, their minds are pitted against their bodies in order to "rid [the female body] of all the desires projected on it" (Bahri 2). In other words, by killing off their bodies with their minds, they simulate their own deaths as a means to give language to "l'irréalité de [leur] existence" (*La Voyeuse interdite* 22).

Cyberspace and Anorexia: Disembodiment as a Form of (Self-) Control

It is widely accepted among the proponents of virtual reality and telecommunications technologies that the body is fast becoming a thing of the past. No longer necessary for travel or even sexual intercourse, the body in the space of the screen is just another cultural artifact in a world that is hailed in much contemporary discourse as a space of revolutionary transformation of the self and identity.

Sherry Turkle's analysis of multi-user games (MUDs or Multi-User Dungeons) on the internet is indicative of the way in which the body is positioned in discourses on cyberspace. MUDs for Turkle "provide worlds for social interaction in a virtual space, worlds in which you can present yourself as a 'character,' in which you can be anonymous, in which you can play a role or roles as close or as far away from your 'real self' as you choose" (158). In these worlds, describes Turkle, "the self is not only decentered but multiplied without limit" (159), and the body is released from its real life limitations as the player engenders a new "ideal" self.

Peter, to use one of Turkle's case studies as an example, is a graduate student who has had heart trouble since childhood. Restricted by his delicate health, he has turned to the MUDs as a means to engage in the types of activities his real body has prevented him from enjoying. In the MUDs, for instance, Peter can frequent a chat group in Germany thereby experiencing the country and its people without risk to his body. Moreover, "[o]n the MUD, Peter shapes a character, Achilles, who is his ideal self. Life in a University of Massachusetts dorm has put him in modest and unaesthetic circumstances. Yet the room he inhabits on the MUD is elegant, romantic, out of a Ralph Lauren ad" (Turkle 162). And to top it off, Peter, "who has known little success with women" in real life, was able on the MUD to charm "Winterlight," one of the three female players who was a "most desirable and sought after player." For Peter, as for many other players, the MUDs are exemplary sites for exploring, constructing, and reconstructing their identities, an aspect Turkle links to the "postmodern ethos of the value of multiple identities" (166).

What concerns me about Turkle's study and others like it is not the appraisal of virtual reality as an "identity workshop." Certainly, cyberspace can be mobilized as a site of cultural struggle, enabling people to move into alternate and potentially empowering subjectivities.[13] What I do find troublesome, however, is the extent to which the privileging of the elements of self-empowerment and self-creation supposedly inherent to these technological mediums obscures the cultural ideologies that inform such practices, as well as the conditions that continue to discipline both material *and* cyber-bodies along the lines of race, class, and gender.[14] Peter's choice of a room that looks like a Ralph Lauren ad and his easily acquired romantic success are revelatory in this regard. Together, these elements suggest a correlation of wealth and male sexual power that is all too often realized in patriarchal cultural contexts at the expense of disempowered groups, especially (black) women and youth.[15] Moreover, they reflect the extent to which media-generated communities (like those of power feminism?) are often "forged out of the empty presence of commodity culture…out of the slogans, signs, headlines and sound bites that structure identity around the quest for global market superiority" (McLaren and Hammer 105). Therefore, while we may agree with Turkle when she hails Peter's constructed environment as personally enabling and radically transformative on the level of his physical disability, this argument is substantially weakened when we take into account the consumerist logic and desire for mastery that inform his alternate reality, not to mention Peter's isolation, if not outright escape, from his body and the "living realm of contact and touch" (Robins 3). For as Peter's case helps us to see, what is at stake in disembodied existence are the very conditions upon which social interaction and exchange are built: encounters with the Other's body. As Robins explains,

> If we experience the world, it is because we are bodily present in it: experience is inherently embodied. It is as embodied beings that we come upon others…. And as embodied beings, we come across others in their difference, others who extend our awareness and experience, but others who also frustrate our expectations or put demands on us. We have to recognise our separation from others…and therefore our dependency on them. This has been the basis of our sociality and this is what we are disavowing in the drive to disembodiment. (32)

In *La Voyeuse interdite*, as we have seen, this type of disembodied existence is actualized in the separation of space into the public (masculine) and the private (feminine). The public space is strictly guarded by the threat of rape since men in this novel consider any woman circulating on the street to be a whore: "On ne pouvait rien dire, les femmes qui sortaient dans la rue étaient des poufiasses!" (22). If a woman is in the street, as the below example demonstrates, she must take guard to efface herself as much as possible. Finally, so as to "protect" women, the decision is made by the men in power to restrict them to the home. The suppression of women from the homogenous masculine sphere is tantamount to the suppression of the Other, a dynamic that is represented by the narrator as a psychosis:

> A la main crispée de ma mère lorsque nous sortions, à ses épaules voûtées afin de dissimuler les moindres attributs féminins, à son regard fuyant devant les hordes d'hommes agglutinés sous les platanes de la ville sale, j'ai vite compris que je devais me retirer de ce pays masculin, ce vaste asile psychiatrique. Nous étions parmi des hommes fous séparés à jamais des femmes par la religion musulmane... (21)

The "drive to disembodiment" prevalent in cyber-rhetoric presents itself here in the guise of religious fundamentalism, for what these two mentalities share is a deep-seated fear of the Other. The Other is this context stands "for that which catastrophically challenges our sense of order and stability" (Robins 27). Like Death, the Other is unknowable and thereby constitutes "the limit of the subject's virility" (Robins 27). In order to suppress this threat, both cyber-dwellers and religious fundamentalists seek to obliterate its source: the Other's body.

The space of the screen thus represents a denial of reality and a cultural *space of refuge*. Because it is a safe place which shelters us from the realities of the body's limitations and needs, it paradoxically stimulates our appetite for such containment even while it eliminates the physicality upon which appetite is built. In other words, as John Berger describes, the more we consume experience through technologically mediated forms, the more our bodies disappear, effacing in the process the corporeal dimensions of existence:

> L'innovation technologique a rendu aisée la séparation de l'apparence et de l'existant. Et c'est précisément ce que la mythologie a besoin d'exploiter en permanence. Il transforme les apparitions en réfractions, comme des mirages: non des réfractions de lumière, mais d'appétits, en fait un seul appétit, l'appétit d'avoir plus. Il en résulte—paradoxe, étant données les implications physiques de la notion d'appétit—que l'existant, le corps disparaît. Nous vivons au sein d'un spectacle de vêtements vides et de masques flottants. ("Un système" 97)

The alliance of appetite with the consumption of new, technologically mediated (i.e. safe) life styles[16] which supersede the body is not without relevance to contemporary manifestations of anorexia nervosa among young women. Let me first point out that in making this connection, I am in no way suggesting that anorexia nervosa is *caused* by technoculture. Rather, following Bordo, I am implying that the contemporary "drive to disembodiment" and its correlative erasure of the body's limitations and needs have contributed to a cult of bodily control whose ultimate female practitioner is the anorectic.[17] As Bordo writes,

> [t]he spread of eating disorders, of course, is not just about images. The emergence of eating disorders is a complex, multilayered cultural 'symptom,' reflecting problems that are historical as well as contemporary, arising in our time because of the confluence of a number of factors. Eating disorders are overdetermined in this culture. They have to do not only with new social expectations of women and ambivalence toward their bodies but also with more general anxieties about the body as the source of hungers, needs, and physical vulnerabilities not within our control. These anxieties are deep and long-standing in Western philosophy and religion, and they are especially acute in our own time. Eating disorders are also linked to the contradictions of consumer culture, which is continually encouraging us to binge on our desires at the same time as it glamorizes self-discipline and scorns fat as a symbol of laziness and lack of willpower. And these disorders reflect, too, our increasing fascination with the possibilities of reshaping our bodies and selves in radical ways, *creating new bodies according to our mind's design.* (*Twilight Zones* 112, my emphasis)

The anorectic, in her pursuit of absolute control over the body's hunger,[18] can be said to allegorically represent the mind/body dualism enacted in the larger cultural arena of consumerism and cyberspace (itself dominated to a large degree by masculinist assumptions). In her attempts to attain absolute self-sufficiency by denying the need for external objects (for example food and bodily contact with others),[19] the anorectic lives a form of virtual subjectivity much like that to be found in cyberspace. In both cases, despite substantive differences in terms of the consequences of such perception, reality is artificial: "To interact with it entails suspension of the real and physical self, or its substitution by a disembodied, virtual surrogate or clone. Under these conditions of existence, it appears as if there are no limits to what can be imagined and acted out" (Robins 94). Susan Bordo has described how "the anorectic…literally cannot *see* her body as other than her inner reality dictates" (*Unbearable Weight* 152). Most certainly, for anorectics, who do not choose to perceive reality as artificial, this displacement entails immense physical and mental suffering which is not involved in the experience of virtual subjectivity in cyberspace. I do not wish, under any circumstance, to belittle the anorectic's inability to remove herself from this mindset. Nevertheless, from a cultural perspective, there are some striking similarities between the subjectivites enabled by cyberspace and those described by anorectics.[20] For example, "although the anorectic may come very close to death…the dominant experience throughout the illness is of *invulnerability*" (Bordo, *Unbearable Weight* 153). The dream of immortality is also shared by inhabitants of cyberspace and technoculture, as we have been discussing throughout this study.[21] Furthermore, both anorectics and cyberspace dwellers experience a feeling of intoxication within the worlds they have created, suggesting that the same psychic dramas may be at stake. Consider, for instance, the parallels between the experience of playing video games—which, as Kevin Robins explains, "activate infantile terrors and defences, creating a 'paranoiac environment' in which players are continually and repeatedly struggling to save themselves from being overwhelmed or annihilated by alien, destructive forces" (72)—and the anorectic's experience of her body as alien and outside, a prison from which she must constantly escape (Bordo, *Unbearable Weight* 147).[22] Just as image and virtual reality technologies deliver subjects "from the constraints and defeats of physical reality and the physical body" (Robins 89), then, so does the anorectic's self-starvation distance her from her real-world body in order to overcome its physicality. Both phenomena, moreover, lead the subject to experience a certain exhilaration that "comes from the sense of transcendence and liberation from the material and embodied world" (Robins 88).[23]

The reader may object that my presentation of anorexia nervosa as the manifestation of a particularly female form of disembodied subjectivity— akin to those subjectivities enacted in the larger consumer culture driven by conflictual (often masculinist) presentations of gender—is overly attached to the processes of "westernization." However, as Melanie Katzman and Sing Lee point to, "simply viewing eating disorders as a Western culture-bound syndrome 'rooted in Western cultural values and conflicts'" is highly problematic (387). Indeed, their study, which examines cases of eating disturbance in both Eastern and Western societies, "demonstrate[s] the ways in which women straddling two worlds, be it generational, work-family, cultural, or traditional and modern, may employ food denial as a instrumental means of negotiating the transition, disconnection, and oppression they uniformly endure" (385). Therefore, far from representing a specifically "Western" form of female experience and subjectivity, anorexia nervosa must be acknowledged as a specific and gendered embodiment of power differentials (Katzman and Lee 385) which find different means of expression throughout a broad array of cultural practices.

Having drawn some parallels that link seemingly disparate cultural manifestations of disembodiment, I want now to sharpen my focus to discuss anorexic disembodiment in *La Voyeuse interdite*. I seek to illustrate the extent to which Bouraoui presents anorexia nervosa as a manifestation of cultural resistance to "a socio-sexual code that is designed to prepare [women] for an unequal marriage market while repressing her sexuality" (Bahri 2). In addition, I suggest that anorexia serves as an allegory of memory, a figuration of the cultural silencing of women and the reduction of their bodies to mere tropes (Purity; Death; Nature) in the service of both nationalist and patriarchal modes of thought and representation.

Anorexia and Amnesia: Women and Memory in Nina Bouraoui

"All profound changes in consciousness, by their very nature, bring with them characteristic amnesias. Out of such oblivions, in specific historical circumstances, spring narratives." Thus does Benedict Anderson describe the process whereby identity is formed, a figuration of personal or national History which, "because it can not be 'remembered,' must be narrated" (204). For Fikria, the young woman "cachée derrière sa fenêtre" looking out onto the streets of Algeria in the guise of "la voyeuse interdite," the amnesia out of which all writing and all identity is born takes the form of a lie:[24]

> Le mensonge s'insurge un jour dans votre vie. Difficile de savoir. Balancier infatiguable, il cogne entre les deux sphères opposées, rebondit sur le plus puis sur le moins mais c'est toujours la vitre du réel qui se brise en premier, et nous nous laissons alors déporter par notre propre jeu vers un voyage sans valise. Ma rue est le support de l'aventure, la trame, l'obscur tableau où s'incrit une prose indéchiffrable pour le badaud. Il faut prendre le temps d'observer, ne pas côtoyer sans voir, ne pas effleurer sans saisir, ne pas cueillir sans sentir, ne pas pleurer sans aimer ni haïr. L'important est l'histoire. *Se faire une histoire de regarder le vrai. Réelle, irréelle, qu'importe! Le récit entoure la chose d'un nouvel éclat, le temps y dépose un de ses attributs privilégiés, mémoire, souvenir ou réminiscence, le hasard peaufine l'oeuvre et la chose prend forme.* (11, my emphasis)

The "amnesic memory"[25] that is common to the construction of historical, national, and personal identity is invoked here in the young sequestered girl's vision of her street, for it is here that the story of her "coming of age" and forced marriage—her sacrifice—will indeed unfold. Significantly, however, the story she will tell is not hers alone; for in recounting the story of her adolescence, she gives voice not only to "ces filles des maisons voisines" but also to her mother, her sisters Zohr and Leyla, her aunt Kadidja and her daughter Rime, Ourdia, a desert nomad, and finally to her country, Algeria, whose "body" (the street) is inseparable from the narrator's: "Je ne pourrai jamais quitter ma rue. *Je fais corps avec elle comme je fais corps avec ces filles des maisons voisines.* Chaque nuit, à tour de rôle, compagnes fidèles sans nom ni visage, nous nourrissons nos âmes d'un nouvel élan strictement spirituel..." (11, my emphasis).[26] By linking her body with both the bodies of other women and the nation itself, Fikria explicitly foregrounds the female body as a site for the construction and reproduction of nationalist ideologies. In the following passage, which transforms Algeria literally into the (maternal) body of a woman, she further establishes a continuum between Woman as allegory of the nation and women as markers of cultural intercourse:

Ma ville est une vieille séductrice endormie, le souffle lent, le rêve audible mais poussif, elle sommeille au bord du lit de ses premières amours. Amants de passage, maîtresses possessives, maris jaloux, soupirants timides et jeunes filles éprises de Beauté ont couvert son corps de fleurs et de baisers, encensé son âme d'admiration et de respect. Insoumise, généreuse, grande amoureuse, ivre de Vie et de bonheur, amante comblée et affectueuse, elle fut au centre des dîners fermés l'emblème de la grâce, l'intérêt de la presse mondaine, l'enthousiasme des hommes, des femmes et des enfants. Congratulée dans les dîners protocolaires, effigie de la planète entière, sacrée par les dieux et les déesses de l'Antiquité, ministres, reines, rois, princes et princesses, présidents, ducs et baronnes, démocrates et dictateurs ont étreint son corps.... *Muse, modèle, savante un peu folle, mère nourricière, amoureuse grisée, elle fut le berceau des audaces, de la joie et de la gloire; écrivains, poètes, peintres, sculpteurs, s'endormaient dans le creux de son ventre*: la fameuse baie d'Alger. (69, my emphasis)

"Beauté;" "Vie;" "Muse:" All the classical tropes of femininity are summoned here as a means of highlighting women's status as icons and bearers of culture. Nevertheless, in her role as the "voyeuse interdite," Fikria successfully inscribes herself in the interstices of the culture/nature dualism. For in speaking the story of her own and other women's submission to the (reproductive) body, "the social construction of the feminine self, fixed by a masculine gaze, is both confirmed and ironised, because the body, as site for this social inscription, is self-consciously present. The woman [speaking] shows herself as subject and object of her representation of woman as sign; of woman positioned by gender and by death" (Bronfen 407). In *La Voyeuse interdite*, this double inscription takes on added significance since the narrator tells her story despite the fact that she is forcibly forbidden by her father to speak: "aucune parole, aucun regard ne trahit le silence un peu solennel imposé par l'homme de la maison" (23). This imposed silence, which extends to all women and even to the streets of Algeria itself, is presented in *La Voyeuse interdite* through a specifically female lineage. For within the context of Islamic fundamentalism which frames this narrative, as Wassyla Tamzali points to, "women symbolize tradition and cultural identity. It is as if the whole burden of the Islamic tradition rests on their shoulders" (qtd. in M. Simons, *New York Times*). The fundamentalist targeting of women's bodies as a means to articulate and enforce (whether by dress or by rape) religious cultural identity (an identity that is perceived as "threatened" in the context of globalization) has meant turning back the clock on women's rights in many contexts. In *La Voyeuse interdite*, as we see in the below example, these tensions are enacted through the bodies of young women, a cultural imposition that is represented by the narrator as an allegorization (suppression) of women's bodies (they represent Purity) toward the repression not only of their voices and presence in public, but also of their (sexual) desire:

> Adolescentes, vous vivez dans l'ombre d'une déclaration fatale, votre jeunesse est un long procès qui s'achèvera dans le sang, un duel entre la tradition et votre pureté. Pures trop impures! franchement vous ne faites pas le poids! pensez au lourd fardeau du temps qui entraîne inlassablement dans son cycle infernal des torrents de règles, de coutumes, de souvenirs, de réflexes, d'habitudes, des torrents de boue dans lesquels s'ensevelit votre sexe déjà coupable à la naissance. Gouffre de l'a priori et de l'inné! Qui doit payer? Vous, grand-mères au doigt inquisiteur, détective de fautes et de souillures…. Nous, les duplicatas exacts de la première génération, pécheresses passives et soumises! toi drap maculé de sang et d'honneur? *Dans ton tissu se dessine à l'encre carmin l'espoir et la crainte des mères, des pères, de l'homme, de la patrie, de l'histoire!…la pureté ne se borne pas à un dérisoire écoulement de sang!* La nuit le rideau se déchire et je les entends ces hyènes affamées, ces prétendues figures de vertu!…nos plaintes narguent la jeunesse de la rue sans femme… (13–14, my emphasis)

Refusing to occupy the honorary space allotted her by patriarchal narratives, in which she is required to preserve her virginity as a symbol of male honor, the narrator cries out for a specifically female revolution. In a direct address to her female compatriots, she beseeches: "Descendez de vos tanières, ne perdons plus notre temps et le leur, désorientons avec courage le cours de la tradition, nos moeurs et leurs valeurs, arrachons rideaux et voiles pour joindre nos corps" (14)! This cry, however, is as sterile as the narrator's existence, resounding as it does only between the walls of her "cellule" where she will remain imprisoned until her (forced) marriage, or what she refers to as "la nuit de [s]es noces sanglantes." As she remarks in the following passage, verbal and emotional protestation make no sense in a context where women's voices are cloistered, fragmented, and subordinated to the transmission of patriarchal cultural mythology which, in its recourse to tradition, appropriates female bodies to preserve itself:

> A quoi bon? Mes larmes n'entendraient que l'écho de larmes identiques espacées par le jeu des murs et de l'horizon restreint. Je suis mon propre écho, mon propre interlocuteur, ma propre tristesse!.... La tendresse, la joie, ou la pitié sont scalpées par le regard inquisiteur de mon père et la haine de ma mère. Les rares éclats de rire ou de désespoir s'en vont vite rejoindre derrière un meuble les poussières du quotidien; là, entre le bois et le plâtre, se meurent nos tentatives d'émotion. Je n'ose parler d'amour. Invention insensée, miasme importé d'Occident, illusion mensongère, perversion de la jeunesse! chez nous, pas de hasard, pas d'émoi, pas de rencontre.... On trace votre courbe d'"amour," impossible de s'en écarter, elle coupe le passage à toute pénétration qui l'éloignerait de sa finalité. Tout est prêt. Il suffit de choisir le moment propice. Qui parle de destin? (63)

Effectively buried, then, in a society that offers women little opportunity for self-determination beyond the acceptance of her (corporeal) role as mother and wife, the "voyeuse" turns to the only other solution imaginable: death. Yet her death is not limited to the one assigned to her in masculine culture. Far from embodying allegorically Beauty, Purity, Innocence, or Muse, Fikria takes the cultural ideology that assigns female flesh to excess and death quite literally and sets about trying to release her mind from her decaying body through the enactment of her own symbolic death:

> Le silence, la solitude, l'abandon définitif de la Vie vraie me submergent d'une peur inhumaine, les autres se taisent, les murs se rapprochent, mon corps est à la limite de la putréfaction. Je sens mes organes durcir, et le coeur décide, seul, d'un nouveau tempo: la petite musique de la mort. Poussée par l'instinct de survie je chasse la décadence par la décadence, le mal et le mal se suffisant à eux-mêmes se retournent brusquement vers le bien, et, par la douleur de l'interdit, je réveille mon corps, le sauve in extremis de la chute, le couvre de pensées meurtrières et je m'enfante moi-même! (43)

As this example demonstrates, Fikria embraces death as a means by which to re-create her self. In so doing, she is following the example of her anorexic sister Zohr who is already well advanced into the deterioration brought about by self-starvation and denial:

> Fait d'un seul bloc dont on distingue à peine le profil de la face, le corps chétif de Zohr est amputé des deux sculptures majestueuses que Dieu nous a confiées en toute innocence. Tous les soirs, elle resserre un savant corset de bandelettes qui masque deux seins dont les pointes sans support suffoquent derrière la bande de tissu close par une épingle à nourrice, elle-même logée dans la ridicule rigole séparant les deux pousses qui n'arriveront jamais à terme. Elle ne défait son corset que pour frictionner son torse semblable à un dos dont les omoplates seraient marquées par deux taches brunes au relief énigmatique. Rougi par la gaze nouée à même la peau, ce tronc entravé reste cependant droit, ne trahissant jamais la ligne parfaitement horizontale des jambes jointes à un bassin sans hanche.... *Zohr est en guerre contre sa nature, nature féminine, pourriture pour notre père, honte pour notre fautive de mère...* (27, my emphasis)

Zohr's portrait recalls a characteristic fear of adolescent anorectics: "to be mature, sexually developed, and potentially reproductive women" (Bordo, *Unbearable Weight* 155). Indeed, as Fikria's comments in the following example suggest, it is only a matter of time before she herself will turn to self-starvation. However, for the time being, it is she who will be required to take Zohr's place as the first to be married:

> Décédée depuis longtemps de l'intérieur, desséchée de l'extérieur, je suis comme toi Zohr! tu as juste un peu d'avance ajoutée à la pratique, c'est tout! La vie est une voleuse. J'ai dérobé ta place, revêtu tes vêtements, j'ai fait de ta peau ma peau, de ton sexe, mon sexe. Plus âgée, siyed Bachir aurait dû pointer son index sur toi. (132)

Earlier in this chapter, I discussed anorexia as a specifically female form of self-determination akin to certain types of identity transformation available in the space of virtual reality. I suggested that anorexia, like "power feminism" and the "drive to disembodiment" prevalent in cyberspace and televisual culture, is a specific cultural practice that seeks to deny the body so as to transcend the constraints of the material world. For women, this transcendence is highly problematic due to their cultural positioning in the (maternal/sexualized) body, a position that is associated with powerlessness. Hence self-starvation as a means to control this situation, a phenomenon that helps to explain why anorexia is predominantly a female malady: in order for women to transcend the constraints of the material world, they must also transcend their bodies. This scenario is illustrated by Fikria and Zohr as they establish control over their bodies in a gesture of denial toward the system that seeks to commodify them through marriage. In this sense, anorexia nervosa—far from existing as a totally Western paradigm associated mainly with beauty ideals transmitted by the media and a fear of fat[27]—represents "a fairly universal difference for males and females in the task of establishing self-definition and self-control" (Katzman and Lee 389).[28]

In *La Voyeuse interdite*, the manifestation of anorexia nervosa as a struggle for self-determination in the face of power imbalances (themselves structured along the lines of gender) is presented through the abhorration or denial of feminine traits such as menstruation and developed breasts. The narrator, for example, represents the onset of her menstrual cycles as the invasion of her body by an alien force: "Un étranger me tailladait le sexe de l'intérieur, je me transformais en une monstrueuse insulte et priais Dieu de toutes mes forces pour qu'il arrêtât cet écoulement ignoble et ignominieux!" (32). Moreover, women's breasts are repeatedly represented as a sign of monstrosity and repulsion: "tous ces seins ballottant avec la disgrâce des monstres me donnent la nausée" (87). Zohr, as we have seen, delays the onset of womanhood interminably by wrapping her chest so tightly, her breasts simply cannot grow.

As these examples point to, anorexia nervosa in Bouraoui's texts has everything to do with "fear and disdain for traditional female roles and social limitations," especially reproduction (Bordo, *Unbearable Weight* 155). This fear springs from the "non-existence" of women in society, especially in this text where women are cloistered from puberty until marriage in order to safeguard their virginity and "honor." It is also linked to the failure of their own mother to produce a son, the ultimate sign of acceptance and validation for women in *La Voyeuse interdite*. In fact, Zohr's anorexia is presented by "la voyeuse" as specifically linked to her mother's shame, for as she tells us, their mother is la traîtresse qui pousse Zohr toujours plus loin dans ses sacrifices, ses artifices et ses dissimulations grotesques. Et la diaphane n'oublie jamais en notre présence de pincer sa bouche légèrement charnue une fois relâchée, pour cacher, mordre au sang, détruire enfin ce bout de chair rouge et strié, signe de vie et de fécondité! (28)

Here, in the metaphorical association between the tongue and the clitoris, the mouth and the vagina, Bouraoui explicitly articulates the loss of voice and control that accompanies the supression of female *jouissance* and appetite for life when women are expected (or coerced whether by force or by lack of acceptable alternatives) to follow the paths society and (male) culture have traditionally designated as "feminine."[29] Zohr, for her part, will escape her destiny since she has already chosen death as her partner in marriage. In the following passage, the excessively corpulent tante K. has come for a visit.[30] Acting as an accomplice and surrogate archetypal Mother, she turns her eyes to Zohr, searching for signs of her future:

Elle trouve Zohr encore amaigrie, lui reproche ses côtes, ses veines trop voyantes, son dos ailé et ses genoux tremblants. Tu ne trouveras jamais de mari, Zohr! vieille fille! voilà ce que tu es, une vieille fille indécente! comment peut-on se laisser dépérir ainsi? qui voudra de toi ma pauvre enfant avec tes yeux cerclés de noir et tes mains de squelette?! Zohr ne dit rien, elle se contente de sourire puis ferme son poing gauche pour cacher un anneau invisible: son alliance avec la Mort. (86)

Zohr's anorexia, like the image in Blanchot's sense, places her into a liminal position between the living and the dead (she is in fact a macabre allegory of the cultural conjunction between femininity and death, that "cadaverous presence"),[31] a space from which she can form an alternative subjectivity. Yet, as Bronfen's analysis of the "dead bride" suggests, this position, is ultimately ambiguous:

What remains open to debate...is whether the bride's death is a moment of real subjectivity because it reflects the choice of her fate, or whether it is the acme of her social victimization. The former case implies that death is a moment of subjectivity because it engenders a destruction of the gendered body, which, were the bride to accept it, would also mean accepting the constraints culture requires of the 'mature' feminine position. *Destroying her body is coterminous with destroying the site at which culture locates the curtailment of her subjectivity.* In other words, these representations of the 'dead bride' raise the question whether the position ascribed to fulfilled femininity is a form of psychic death or whether death is the only agency of real feminine power and self-articulation. (270, my emphasis)

When we consider the case of self-starvation, which frequently "symbolizes a loss of voice in a social world perceived to be solely oppressive" (Katzman and Lee 388), it becomes clear that the battle women wage over the body is a concrete (though indirect) expression of the female subject's will to dominate the obstacles that prevent her self-realization. For "la voyeuse interdite," who presents herself throughout the narrative as Zohr's double, dominating her body through acts of the mind (including surmounting the pain of self-inflicted wounds and bodily mutilations)[32] becomes a ritualistic practice which allows her to become simultaneously subject (male) and object (female) of representation. Locked in her room, staring out the window, which takes on the allure of "l'écran muet de la télévision" (26), "elle avait cultivé...la fleur de l'observation et par une curieuse osmose ratifiée par le pacte du sang, elle devenait elle-même objet, chose, matière" (104). Significantly, equipped with this double vision, the narrator is able to maintain herself in a position between life and death, or childhood and womanhood:

> Vieille adolescente fripée avant l'âge, ma silhouette et mon visage ne sont pas restés fidèles à mes photos d'enfant, seuls les yeux sont intacts avec un cerne supplémentaire qui rappelle joliment leur noir encre. Bique au poil trop long qui joue du sabot en attendant qu'on l'arrache du troupeau pour l'abattoir, je vis ma jeunesse sur le fil du rasoir, un faux pas, un seul signe et je suis bonne pour l'événement. Manie de famille, je commence à dissimuler mes seins en me tenant légèrement courbée, les côtes rentrées et les bras en bouclier. *Le corps et le pire des traîtres, sans demander l'avis de l'intéressé, il livre bêtement à des yeux étrangers des indices irréfutables: âge, sexe, féconde pas féconde?* Pubère, il m'a rendue inapprochable, dans le royaume des hommes je suis LA souillure, sur l'échiquier des dames, le pion en attente caché derrière une reine hautaine qui choisira seule le bon moment pour se déplacer.... *Pour l'instant, j'arrive à me dédoubler: je suis pion et joueuse à la fois. Concentration. Sur moi, les choses, la rue. Je suis capable de rester plusieurs heures assise dans ma chambre avec un seul objectif: contorsionner mon esprit.* Les

yeux jouent un rôle secondaire, la pensée, chef d'orchestre de l'opération, occupe la totalité du champ plane et sans encombre. (61, my emphasis)

In this example, Fikria's window—the space of the screen—enables her to engender herself as the subject of her story, despite the fact that her body betrays her by telling the only story—the "true" story (age, sex, fertility)— that matters for women in this book. On the one hand, then, this space holds the promise of liberty and escape for it allows the narrator to experiment with her identity and to stake out a feminine subject position, as the following description of what the narrator experiences in front of her window demonstrates:

> Dominatrice des Mauresques, porte-parole du silence, maîtresse des Hommes et des choses, la rue, la ville, le monde m'appartient! je suis la veine centrale de l'événement, le premier moteur des êtres, la libératrice des citadelles d'antan, la Cassandre du nouveau siècle! Je détiens la perspective, maintiens l'horizon et rien n'échappe à mes pinceaux marron, supports sensibles de l'émotion. (99)

Here, it is Fikria who controls not only her own destiny, but also all the events that make up her history. However, on the other hand, as we have already pointed out, the space of the screen cannot safeguard the narrator from the role her body plays in the "real world," that is to say "food" off which the cultural subjugation of women feeds. It therefore provides only a brief respite from an otherwise unappealing reality.

Thus can we explain the metaphorical associaton of food and the female body throughout *La Voyeuse interdite*, as well as the subsequent turn to anorexia by the young women to "remedy" (i.e. control) their position as future victims for the slaughter (symbolized in this text as forced marriage and reproduction). Throughout the narrative, "la voyeuse" associates women with fleshy animals or objects (her mother is "une outre grasse…beuglant comme un animal traqué" (36–37)) destined to be devoured by men. In the following passage, which exploits the well-worn cliché that pairs female body parts with fruit, the narrator's father eats some grapes, an act which is presented as a sexual violation by the narrator:

> Pointillés de petits pores dilatés, ses doigts tripotent une grappe de muscat. Les grains enflés de sucre roulent, glissent puis crèvent sous la

pression du pouce et de l'index...un des grains éventrés...crache son jus et ses pépins sur le rebord de la table basse. Avec sa peau fine et transparente, le fruit troué ressemble à mon sexe d'adolescente, attaché à la branche principale par deux ramifications qui pourraient être mes jambes, il vide sa chair devant mon père. (31)

Moreover, when women themselves eat in the narrative, the narrator experiences their appetitie as a "deep fear of 'the Female,' with all its more nightmarish archetypal associations of voracious hungers and sexual insatiability" (Bordo, *Unbearable Weight* 155), a fear that is commonly evoked by anorexic women. Consider, for example, the description of the feast that takes place on the narrator's wedding night, in which she metaphorically and poetically joins the image of a stuffed roast sheep with that of (pregnant and/or hetero/sexually active) women—here presented as vultures—who are about to eat it.

> Allongé sur un lit de pommes de terre, d'ail, de persil et d'herbes rouges, jambes en l'air, cuisses immobiles, sexes farcis, ventre béant et yeux mi-clos, graisse cirée et chair généreuse, le méchoui attend les doigts dévastateurs.... Telles des poupées mécaniques, les valseuses quittent le socle tournant pour remettre leurs chaussures; les doigts dévastateurs s'échauffent en claquant l'air d'un air enjoué et s'accrochent au buffet sanglant: la chasse est déclarée ouverte!.... Les mains expertes saluent au passage les têtes criblées d'ail pour se disculper, plongent dans une coupelle d'eau sacrée puis se balancent dans le vide comme les ailes d'un vautour au-dessus des cercueils ouverts; impatients mais gênés par l'abondance, les doigts dévastateurs bénissent les chairs étalées, mortes, gisantes dans la sauce...indécent festin dans le pays du manque, indécence d'une tombe violée.... [C]roqueuses de morts, les Mauresques affairées mastiquent les viandes trop cuites et d'un coup de langue fourchue, elles happent les petits bouts de cadavres accrochés à leurs lèvres 'pneumatiques.' Agglutinées autour du cercueil rectangulaire, elles se bousculent, lèchent, trouent, déglutissent, s'étouffent, arrachent, cisaillent, sucent, s'aspergent, découpent, s'abreuvent, et dans un rot commun, elles digèrent la mort! (133–137)

Comparing the feasting women to grave robbers, the bodies over which these women are indulging are equivalent to those of the young girls who are sacrificed in this text as so many lambs for the sake of tradition.[33]

Here, "la voyeuse" speaks on behalf of the voiceless daughters to express the rage they feel at being "mutilated" and reduced to silence. As Adrienne Rich explains,

> [m]any daughters live in rage at their mothers for having accepted, too readily and passively, 'whatever comes.' A mother's victimization does not merely humiliate her, it mutilates the daughter who watches her for clues as to what it means to be a woman. Like the traditional foot-bound Chinese woman, she passes on her own affliction. The mother's self-hatred and low expectations are the binding-rags for the psyche of the daughter. (*Of Woman Born* 243)

Nira Yuval-Davis has similarly described how compliant behaviour of women reproduces the national collectivity culturally, since "women are often the ones chosen to be the intergenerational transmitters of cultural tradtions, customs, songs, cuisine, and, of course, the mother tongue (*sic*)" (198). In *La Voyeuse interdite*, the enactment of the daughter's rage toward the mother's transmission of powerlessness manifests itself as a disgust toward food, female flesh, and the role of the female in heterosexual coupling and reproduction. It is not by coincidence, moreover, that the daughter identifies her mother with the realm of the house that most closely suggests her domestic, machine-like function: the kitchen. Moreover, it is here, "dans la petite cuisine aveugle" that the narrator witnesses the source of her mother's greatest humiliation when, after waking from a nap, she goes to the kitchen to get a drink of water. There, she sees her father and her mother "vautrés sur le carrelage," engaged in sexual intercourse:

> Plein d'envies inassouvies, il se vengeait sur le ventre de ma mère en lui administrant des coups violents et réguliers avec une arme cachée dont il était le seul détenteur.... La victime replia ses cuisses monstrueuses.... [A]près une dernière secousse qui ébranla la maison entière, mon père s'arracha du piège visqueux puis se récura les mains avec un savon de ménage. Je voyais sans être vue ma pauvre mère allongée sur le carrelage dont les parties dénudées se couvraient peu à peu de bleus. Mon père parlait fort. Oh oui! il en voulait à ce sexe difforme qui ne lui donnait pas entière satisfaction! pour parfaire son discours peu élogieux il brandit son torchon et la fouetta violemment. Ça se passait toujours ainsi quand ma

mère accouchait. Elle avait à peine le temps de se remettre d'une terrible déception que celui-ci abattait sur elle toute sa rudesse et toute son incompréhension. (38)

In front of her own mother's oppression, and bearing the knowledge that this too, by her own mother's hand, shall be her fate, "la voyeuse" returns in her final hours of youth to the only thing that has properly belonged to her: her room. There, in the space that has constituted her transcendance from her body as she "invented" stories and created herself anew—a space that models the space of the screen—the narrator undertakes the definitive split of mind from body. As she puts on her wedding dress, a garment she associates with the transition of her body from childhood to womanhood and from life to death, the dress becomes her spectral double, "une seconde peau, un double de mon corps qui continuerait à vivre; accrochée à un cintre, *scalpée de sa tête*, animée par des formes vides, imprégnée d'une vieille odeur, je faisais d'elle ma deuxième mémoire" (138, my emphasis). Her room, however—which ironically contains the images of her freedom, that is to say her ability to create an identity beyond the body exterior to the one reserved for her by tradition— will be the guardian of her mind, "ma première peau, mon être et ma respiration" (138). Having effectively severed herself in mind from her body, the narrator can approach her new life with the amnesic memory that characterizes her heritage: "J'ai effacé les dernier vestiges d'un long sanglot, je sais faire les gâteaux, j'ai oublié mes craintes et mon ennui, les fenêtres seront closes, mon esprit aussi, pas de souvenirs, pas de regrets…. J'oublie que je ne suis qu'un ventre reproducteur et je garde précieusement tes bracelets pour mes pauvres petites" (142). As we witness in this scene, and as Bouraoui's representation of the anorectic suggests,

> The reduction of woman to her anatomy produces a curtailment to any definition of a feminine subject position. The urge to destroy the medium through which the destruction of such subjectivity occurs, to undo the site where it is effected and guaranteed, transpires into an urge to obliterate the body itself. *Decorporalization is privileged over an expropriation of her language and her being.* (Bronfen 388–389, my emphasis)

La Voyeuse interdite poses significant challenges to contemporary theories such as those by Turkle which posit the space of the screen as an ideal site for the reconstitution of social identities. For as I hope to have shown in this chapter, even when the space of the screen does facilitate an escape from the limitations posed by physical appearance—allowing for the construction of different identities in the process—the cultural positionings of the body in the real world can all but drown out these transformations. Where women are concerned, this problematic takes on additional dimensions, since the attainment of a feminine subject position in globalized technoculture is often pursued to the detriment of women's health, both psychological and physical. As Adrienne Rich describes and as *La Voyeuse interdite* suggests, to deny the cultural significance and symbolization of our physicality is to profoundly deny our experience and our history:

> [T]he fear and hatred of our bodies has often crippled our brains...the scholar reading denies at her peril the blood on the tampon; the welfare mother accepts at her peril the derogation of her intelligence. These are issues of survival, because the woman scholar and the welfare mother are both engaged in fighting for the mere right to exist. Both are 'marginal' people in a system founded on the traditional family and its perpetuation.... Many women see any appeal to the physical as a denial of the mind. We have been perceived for too many centuries as pure Nature, exploited and raped like the earth and the solar system; small wonder if we now long to become Culture: pure spirit, mind. Yet it is precisely this culture and its political institutions which have split us off from itself. (285)

Anorexia is only one of the many cultural practices that illustrate women's continual negotiation with their prescribed social roles. Yet as it becomes increasingly prevalent in our globalized societies, we must recognize the cultural structures that underwrite its etiology. Bouraoui's representation of the anorectic requires us to view this condition in light of the *range* of sociocultural influences that are disempowering to women across cultures. Such an undertaking, unlike the virtual solutions offered by technoculture, can occur only by forging new relationships both with our own *and* others' bodies, leading to what Katzman and Lee define as "curative cultures:"

> By opening a sociomoral discourse in which the meaning of symptoms can be explored and new social roles forged, groups may provide a forum in which complaints created in the context of relationships can be healed as new social ties evolve and new body images are formed. Such mini communities may offer a home for women coming of age while dwelling in a psychological diaspora—endorsing the cultivation of their local worlds of living, not their bodies. (392)

NOTES

1. Danielle Chavy Cooper, in her reviews of Bouraoui for *World Literature in Review*, writes of the "Rimbaldian delirium" of *La Voyeuse interdite*, as well as of Bouraoui's preference for "linguistic word games and striking images in the André Breton manner" (145).

2. Patriarchy, as Griselda Pollock describes, "does not refer to the static, oppressive domination of one sex over another, but to a web of psycho-social relationships which institute a socially significant difference on the axis of sex which is so deeply located in our very sense of lived, sexual, identity that it appears to us as natural and unalterable" (33).

3. For further discussion on how the gaze was structured along the lines of a masculine perception of space in modernity, see Griselda Pollock's chapter "Modernity and the Spaces of Femininity" in *Vision & Difference*, pp. 50–90.

4. As Teresa de Lauretis argues, "the representation of woman as image (spectacle, object to be looked at, vision of beauty—and the concurrent representation of the female body as the locus of sexuality, site of visual pleasure, or lure of the gaze) is so pervasive in our culture that it necessarily constitutes a starting point for any understanding of sexual difference and its ideological effects in the construction of social subjects, its presence in all forms of subjectivity" (qtd. in Bronfen 110). In her inscription of Maghrebian women as "les Mauresques," statues and images, Bouraoui establishes an intertext with exotic Western representations of "Oriental" women, even while she distorts this vision through her portrayal of female bodies as abject.

5. For pertinent discussions of how women symbolize tradition and national and cultural identity in varying contexts, see also "Feminism and Multiculturalism: Some Tensions" by Susan Moller Okin and "Serbian Nationalism: Nationalism of My Own People" by Maja Korac.

6. We recall here that *La Voyeuse interdite* is situated in the timeframe of the seventies, the years following the decolonization of Algeria and its subsequent national upheavals. The narrative is thus framed by the problematics of postcolonialism, such as the quest for (national) identity and the efforts to navigate cultural disparities between tradition and modernity in the wake of colonialism, developments outside the scope of this chapter. My analysis of the book will not be limited therefore to a specifically postcolonial reading. It is

informed, rather, by postmodern and feminist concerns which nevertheless resonate with postcolonial, social, and psychological ones.

7. While Bronfren is referring to the European construction of Woman as Nature in this passage, her description applies not only to women of color throughout the colonized world, but also to men who belong to marginalized groups (i.e. black men and gay men) who are feminized and hypersexualized by cultural norms. Indeed, it would be remiss to view the conflation of Woman with Body as a strictly Western problem. Dr. Ahmad Muhammad Ali, Secretary-General of the Muslim World League, for example, makes the following observations concerning women in a position letter containing "the Islamic view" to Gertrude Mongella, Secretary-General of the UN's Fourth World Conference on Women:

> There is obvious evidence that men and women are biologically meant to serve distinct functions, most decidedly in the area of procreation, and by extension in related areas of family life, involving the care and nurturing of their offspring.... When women stop bringing up children it means the end of the world.... The Conference should adopt resolutions reinforcing laws, institutions, and cultural norms and practices that encourage stable legal marital unions, and equal sharing in child care and household maintenance. Campaign [sic] should be launched against prostitution, exploitation of women's gender for serving commercial entertainment and pleasure purposes, premarital and extramarital sex and promiscuity. A campaign should also be started against homosexuality and regulate abortions.... (*Saudi Gazette*, Sept 1, 1995)

We are certainly not far from "compulsive heterosexuality" here. We should also be alert to the fact that even though certain men may be targets of a feminizing (oppressive) mechanism, they are nevertheless capable of propagating sexist viewpoints (See bell hooks, *Teaching to Transgress*, p. 116). Nor should we overlook women's collusion in oppressive structures. My main goal in pointing to the construction of Woman as Nature (Body) is not to imply a commonality of experience within that construction; rather it is meant to underline the mind/body dualism that has typically been used to differentiate "masculine" and "feminine" spheres of activity across varying cultural contexts.

8. I agree with Susan Bordo when she suggests that "it is crucial to recognize that a staple of the prevailing sexist ideology against which the feminist model protested was the notion that in matters of beauty and femininity, it is women alone who are responsible for their sufferings from the whims and bodily

tyrannies of fashion. According to that idology, men's desires bear no responsibility, nor does the culture that subordinates women's desires to those of men, sexualizes and commodifies women's bodies, and offers them little other opportunity for social or personal power. Rather, it is in Woman's essential feminine nature to be (delightfully if incomprehensibly) drawn to such trivialities and to be willing to endure whatever physical inconvenience is entailed" (22).

9. The concern with the body's shifting meaning in relation to its varied contexts is related to postmodernism's critique of foundationalism and essentialism. See "Social Criticism without Philosophy: An encounter between Feminism and Postmodernism" by Nancy Fraser and Linda J. Nicholson for an account of essentialism in feminism. While the debate on essentialism has been, by and large, productive and (in terms of the heterocentric and racist biases present in much feminist scholarship) necessary, it should be noted that the ensuing privileging of agency and interpretation also has its pitfalls, notably the absence of any cohesive criteria by which to articulate cross-cultural female experience. In this line of thought, see, for example, "Feminism and Multiculturalism: Some Tensions" by Susan Moller Okin. Of course, this is not only specific to feminism. For many pertinent discussions of this problematic as it relates to contemporary culture, see *Counternarratives: Cultural Studies and Critical Pedagogies in Postmodern Spaces* by Henry A. Giroux et al.

10. Certainly, feminism of the sixties and seventies "[s]ubsum[ed] patriarchal institutions and practices under an oppressor/oppressed model which theorize[d] men as possessing and wielding power over women—who [were] viewed correspondingly as themselves power*less*—[a model which] proved inadequate to the social and historical complexities of the situations of men and women" (Bordo, *Unbearable Weight* 23). Despite its view of power as overly monolithic, however, this second-wave feminist movement defined to a large degree the parameters of poststructuralist thought in its critique of the natural body, "femininity," and various other cultural formulations. To dismiss it because it supposedly perpetuates an essentialist vision of women is, in my view, misguided.

11. The considerable cultural debate over the veil, or hijab, as a symbol of Muslim women's oppression/liberation is significant in relation to the privileging of agency in the discourses of "power feminism." As Hamida Ghafour points out in an article for *The Toronto Star*, "it has long been held in North America that wearing a veil is a symbol of the Muslim woman's oppression." Of late, however, "more and more minority women in North America are speaking out about a new definition of feminism that pertains to their own culture. The idea that a woman who wears a veil is liberated in a culture obsessed with defining

women by their sexuality is one such re-definition Muslim women are considering." Ghafour, for her part, does not see the veil as liberatory for, as she writes, "the veil has severely restricted the women who wear them because it is the very nature of the veil that forces women to become sexual creatures.... [A] woman who decides to wear a veil lest anyone think she is erotic has just defined herself by her sexuality.... The sad truth is that in many ways, women in North America are no more liberated than their counterparts in the Middle East because they are all defined by sexuality, however much our culture has changed in the past 20 years." Ghafour is *not* criticizing here Muslim women's efforts to derail unfair stereotypes. She is pointing rather to a larger, systemic problem that effects all women to varying degrees and which is clouded by the rhetoric of choice. For other perspectives related to the veil, see also Joan Treadway's "Muslim Women Fight Stereotypes;" Sultana Yusufali's "My body is my own business;" and Asla Aydintasbas's "Why they can't turn their backs on the veil."

12. In the interest of space, I have presented an overly simplified vision of the evolutions in feminism during the last 20 years. For a more comprehensive viewpoint, see Linda Alcoff's "Cultural Feminism versus Post-Structuralism: The Identity Crisis in Feminist Theory."

13. See Ella Shohat's and Robert Stam's discussion of virtual reality in *Unthinking Eurocentrism*, p. 356.

14. For example, when it came to "gender swapping" (male players playing as female characters and vice versa) in the MUDs, players noticed that "female characters are besieged with attention, sexual advances, and unrequested offers of assistance which imply that women can't do things by themselves" (Turkle 164). Moreover, while virtual worlds technically enable the player's real flesh and blood body to become invisible ("the created character can have *any* physical description and will be responded to *as a function* of that description"), cultural ideology that determines which types of bodies are *desirable* certainly does not benefit from the same free play: "the plain can experience the self presentation of great beauty; the nerdy can be elegant; the obese can be slender" (Turkle 162, my emphasis). Could we imagine a scenario in which the reverse role-play would be enacted? Where the beautiful willingly become plain, where the elegant willingly become nerdy, and where the slender choose to become obese? Herein lies the danger, in my view, of an uncritical acceptance of the revolutionary powers of virtual worlds, especially insofar as women are concerned.

15. For a discussion of the role of the media and its links to global corporate interests in relation to youth violence and identity today, see "Media

Knowledges, Warrior Citizenry, and Postmodern Literacies," by Peter McLaren and Rhonda Hammer.

16. In "Slacking Off: Border Youth and Postmodern Education," Henry Giroux similarly points out how advertisers attempt "to mobilize the desires, identities, and buying patterns" of youth into a "pedagogy of consumption as part of a new way of appropriating postmodern differences" (73).

17. Other contemporary bodily practices that are driven by total mastery of the body are body-building; strict dieting and fitness regimes; surgery as a way of controlling aging and other bodily "defects" such as fat, small breasts, ethnic features other than Anglo, etc. Perhaps the most alarming manifestation of the desire to transcend the body through control besides anorexia nervosa is acts of violence. It is not by coincidence that as technoculture buries everyday lives under the lure of commodity satisfaction, urban and random acts of violence have increased at an alarming rate. Marshall McLuhan had predicted this state of affairs over 20 years ago: "The loss of individual and personal meaning via the electronic media ensures a corresponding and reciprocal violence from those so deprived of their identites; for violence, whether spiritual or physical, is a quest for identity and the meaningful. The less identity, the more violence" (*Forward through the Rearview Mirror* 82).

18. "It is not usually noted, in popular literature on the subject, that anorexic women are as obsessed with *hunger* as they are with being slim. Far from losing her appetite, the typical anorectic is haunted by it—in much the same way that Augustine describes being haunted by sexual desire—and is in constant dread of being overwhelmed by it. Many describe the dread of hunger, 'of not having control, of giving in to biological urge'... (Bordo, *Unbearable Weight* 146).

19. For anorectics, as Hilde Bruch has written, "the avoidance of any sexual encounter, a shrinking from all bodily contact," is characteristic (qtd. in Bordo, *Unbearable Weight* 148). This has been linked to anxiety and guilt over sexual abuse in many cases.

20. From a therapeutic perspective, the interlinking between anorexia nervosa and other cultural practices also seems beneficial. As Melanie Katzman and Sing Lee remark, "The importance of promoting subjective expressions and assuring anorexic patients that their afflictions 'make sense' was demonstrated in one of the few studies that asked patients to evaluate their treatment experience. Previously anorexic women reported that 'being understood' was one of the most important factors for recovery to occur" (387).

21. The dream of immortality is nothing new. "But what is unique to modernity is that the defeat of death has become a scientific fantasy rather than a philosophical or religious mythology. We no longer dream of eternal union with the gods; instead, we build devices that can keep us alive indefinitely, and we work on keeping our bodies as smooth and muscular and elastic at forty as they were at eighteen. We even entertain dreams of halting the aging process completely" (Bordo, *Unbearable Weight* 153). The fantasies entertained in cyberspace can be seen as extensions of these desires as well.

22. Bordo, quoting Hilde Bruch, writes that patients with eating disorders act "as if for them the regulation of food intake was outside [the self]. This experience of bodily sensations as foreign is, strikingly, not limited to the experience of hunger. Patients with eating disorders have similar problems in identifying cold, heat, emotions, and anxiety as originating in the self" (*Unbearable Weight* 147).

23. For the anorectic, the thin body is associated with "absolute purity, hyperintellectuality and transcendence of the flesh" (Bordo, *Unbearable Weight* 148).

24. It is important to note that this "lie" is also that of the Islamic fundamentalists whom Bouraoui is criticizing in this book (see especially p. 22 in reference to this context). For a more complete account of the relation between Bouraoui's novel and the rise of Islamic fundamentalists in Algeria, see Dominique Fisher's article "'Rue du Phantasme': paroles et regard(s) interdits dans *La Voyeuse interdite* de Nina Bouraoui."

25. Dominique Fisher employs this term in relation to the falsification of History both in the context of the Maghreb and Europe. Her discussion is pertinent to Bouraoui's representation of Algeria and women's position in the face of Islamic fundamentalism. She writes: "Amnesic memory is the touchstone upon which the eradication of women and intellectuals as others, strangers, is implemented.... Indeed, the elimination of strangers, women, or intellectuals, is far from being a new phenomenon, it is merely a repetition of khalifal despotism" ("The Blank Spaces of Interculturality" 92).

26. As Dominique Fisher writes, "Le dire des femmes, dans ce face-à-face masqué du mensonge...que met en spectacle [la narratrice], fait entrer la narration dans un irréel vrai. Ainsi, le dire de la 'voyeuse interdite,' par à-coups, au rythme de la colère, n'hésite pas à glisser dans la polyphonie du 'nous' (les femmes) et la conscience collective" ("'Rue du Phantasme': paroles et regard(s) interdits dans *La Voyeuse interdite* de Nina Bouraoui" 47).

27. As Katzman and Lee argue, "an overreliance on a fear of fatness as a diagnostic feature may result in a failure to recognize anorexia nervosa in broader cultural settings" and could even be interpreted as a Eurocentric mode of thought since, in its focus on "youth, whiteness, thinness, and wealth," it "risks being unduly ethnocentric and misses the universal power of food refusal as an attempt to free oneself from the control of others" (389).

28. This theorization bears itself out in *La Voyeuse interdite* when we consider that even though young men are presented equally in this book as "prisonniers de la ville" without a future, they nevertheless have recourse to the control of women to provide themselves with self-determination and a superior position in society.

29. A striking example of this dynamic is given by Susan Moller Okin in relation to girls and women in Ultra-Orthodox Judaism. As she writes, "girls and women in Ultra-Orthodox Judaism are held responsible for male sexual self-control. Not only are they required to dress 'modestly,' from very early childhood, and to shave or clip short their hair and cover it from the time of puberty. *Even their voices are (in Margalit's words) 'considered sexual organs,' such that little girls are forbidden to sing in the presence of anyone outside their immediate family*" (9, my emphasis).

30. It is important to note that throughout *La Voyeuse interdite*, female corporeality is associated with decadence, disease, voracious sexuality and food. I will return to these motifs later in the chapter.

31. Here, Zohr can be equated with Eurydice in Blanchot's *L'Espace littéraire*, that is to say an allegory of death to which all art aspires. As Blanchot writes, "elle est, sous un nom qui la dissimule et sous un voile qui la couvre, le point profondément obscur vers lequel l'art, le désir, la mort, la nuit semblent tendre. Elle est l'instant où l'essence de la nuit s'approche comme l'*autre* nuit" (225). Zohr, contrary to Eurydice, however, takes on a critical function vis-à-vis the rhetorical strategy that reduces women to death.

32. The narrator, out of frustration with her situation, mutilates herself: "Je cogne ma tempe gauche contre la poignée de ma fenêtre, le fer résonne dans ma tête mais ça ne suffit pas, l'ouverture ricane de plus belle" (88).

33. I recall here the scene in which the narrator informs us that little girls are killed in the street in front of her window, deaths that come to symbolize the narrator's "murder" as well as the false memories created by the women who barter their daughter's lives in order to gain respect. See *La Voyeuse interdite*, pp. 90–94.

CONCLUSION	**Books and Media: Toward the Emergence of a Postmodern Literacy**

"Today," writes Umberto Eco, "the concept of literacy comprises many media. An enlightened policy of literacy must take into account the possibilities of all these media" ("Afterword" 298). Has the time now come, then, for us to consider the book as a displaced form of communication whose influence is minor in comparison to the electronic discourses that are envisioned as more attractive and respected sources of information (Talens 5)? Perhaps. For in image culture, where knowledge is exchanged in the mode of "informatic simulation" (Talens 7), cyberspace appeals to a new typology of social subjects:

> [I]n the exchange of simulation, the languages as such occupy the place of the community of speakers and undermine the referentiality of discourse so necessary to the rational being. As no one speaks with the person who is listening, and as the existence of an external world is no longer necessary to confront the validity—or the absence of validity—of the flow of meanings, the subject does not find a clear identity facing his/her conversation. From this perspective, the subject of the electronic era cannot base him-/herself on the Cartesian 'I think, therefore I am,' but assumes his fragility with a Lacanian 'they think of me, therefore 'I' is not.' (Talens 13)

This fundamental change of paradigm from representation to simulation has understandably effected a shift in the way "literature" is approached, conceptualized, and even read. But while literature has certainly reached a crossroads, it remains, as I have attempted to demonstrate in my readings of Genet, Guibert, and Bouraoui, an important site for critical reflection on the relation between technology, communication, and culture in the electronic age.

By placing media spectatorship at the center of narrative, Genet, Guibert, and Bouraoui bring into focus how the space of the screen alters our perceptions of death, the body, and our experience of the real world. Moreover, as they "read" the cultural images that are screened in the volatile contexts of war, AIDS, and decolonization through the lens of personal experience, they simultaneously point to dominant (hegemonic) representations and disrupt them through the construction of an "oppositional gaze" which produces "negotiated readings" (Shohat and Stam 349).

Significantly, for Genet, Guibert and Bouraoui alike, the construction of this "oppositional gaze" is synonymous with the projection of "gazes from beyond the grave" or, in other words, the voice of death (Blanchot, *The Work of Fire* 245). In their distinctive ways, as we have elaborated in the preceding chapters, these authors' draw on the space of the screen to reconnect the image to psychic *and* bodily demands, especially those related to death. For Genet, the screening of anonymous bodies mutilated by war enables the narrator to create and re-live his own experience of mourning. For Guibert, using the image to explore personal experience facilitates not only the creation of a new mode of fiction writing, but also the ability to communicate with and about death in ways beyond those recognized by dominant culture. Finally, for Bouraoui, images of veiled women serve to effectively silence and kill the real bodies of women who nevertheless come to life in her narrative of personal and collective persecution.

Indeed, in each of the texts we have discussed in this study, all of which are presentations of real historical or autobiographical moments, the space of the screen transposes itself between the real world and the fictional world, and opens onto a space in which the narrator is able to transform himself or herself into a Blanchotian "cadaverous presence" or a spectral subject, a position that is associated with the realm of fascination and death: between here and nowhere, between reality and fiction, between the real and the simulacrum. As the screen inscribes the dead or dying body at the center of narrative, the narrators are able to efface themselves to take on new identities, simulating in effect their own deaths as they transgress the boundaries between life and death, or reality and the image. The readers/spectators, because they identify with the narrator's perspective, are also forced into a "kind of dress-rehearsal for death" as they too adopt this alternate consciousness (McHale 231).

Throughout this study, I have suggested that it is precisely this ability to efface oneself in reality and to project oneself into an alternate world that links literary space to cyberspace in contemporary culture. However, as I have also maintained, while cyberspace and literary space converge in their capacity to produce multiple forms of knowledge and subjectivity, they also differ radically insofar as death is concerned.

We have seen that in contemporary technoculture, death is rendered as a virtual (disembodied) reality and therefore a reality that can be changed and maybe even avoided (whether it be in cyberspace or through the artifice of plastic surgery or medical technologies). Images in this realm are linked to technological rationalization, and spectatorship revolves not around an imaginative space of reflection but rather around the sensation of the spectacle:

> In the case of electronic images…[t]he imaginative space of representation is replaced by the (euphoric) immediacy of presence and experience. Distance is achieved only through the muting of sensation, through the anaesthetisation of the senses. Pain is deferred through the derealisation and devitalisation of the image…. There is no place for perspective, only the possibility of modulating intensity of affect. (Robins 142)

Literary space, on the other hand, is constituted of the very elements that are disavowed in the space of the screen: death and a confrontation with the unknown. We recall that for Blanchot, and as we have seen with Genet, Guibert, and Bouraoui, literary space is made up precisely of exchanges between the living and the dead, since death is that which brings forth the "presence as absence that fictions embody" (Bronfen 349). In this sense, literature may be seen as the cultural space *par excellence* for the resurrection of the dead. For as it creates a space of imaginative reflection anchored precisely in the interstices of life and death, literature enables us to experiment with imagining our own deaths, to rehearse our own deaths... [It] may be one of our last resources for preparing ourselves, in imagination, for the single act which we must assuredly all perform unaided, with no hope of doing it over if we get it wrong the first time. (McHale 232)

This possibility of simulating death for the use of the imagination, as Brian McHale has argued, may very well be the most important and valuable function of the literary text today. For in bringing the image back into contact with death, literary texts such as those written by Genet, Guibert, and Bouraoui also bring readers/spectators back into touch with the unknown (which can also be seen as the Other, alterity, or the Stranger). They thus oppose the logic of rational mastery that frequently modulates the use and deployment of images today. Indeed, by locating the image within the sensual realm of bodily experience, which we have explored through the representation of death and the body, Genet, Guibert, and Bouraoui resist the contemporary mode of "death-defying simulation" which is connected to fantasies of rational transcendence (Robins 161). Their texts work precisely against the bodiless subject of the simulacrum by providing a theoretical space within which alterity, "the otherness that constitutes us[,]...freely circulates through a texture that, paraphrasing Roland Barthes, will no longer be 'dominated by the [technocratic] superego of continuity, a superego of evolution, history [and] filiation'" (Talens 21).

By reconnecting us to death, then, literature maintains its political function for it creatively disrupts technoculture's "ways of seeing" to recover an openness to the world, an openness which entails an *imaginative confrontation* with the Other. The work of Genet, Guibert, and Bouraoui brings about this confrontation by highlighting the space of the screen as a "discursive battle zone" wherein spectators shape and are shaped by their experience with the various media that comprise image culture (Shohat and Stam 349).

Today, we might easily be drawn into thinking in terms that oppose digital forms of communication to the types of print communication represented by the book. Yet clearly, as Robins suggests, "[w]e should aspire to be open to the force of *all* modes of visual representation and presentation," including writing and books (166, my emphasis). The question, in this sense, is not whether digital technologies and their cultural tenets have *replaced* print culture. What is significant, rather, is the extent to which "[t]he coexistence of different images, different ways of seeing, different visual imaginations, may be seen as an imaginative resource" (Robins 165).

Undoubtedly, a different order of imagining is beginning to arise in what we now commonly refer to as the "digital age." With its emphasis on image and digital technologies, as well as the manipulation of "information," the cultural landscape today is dominated by the search for "new" electronic forms. Whether "literature" will be preserved within this order is a question that must remain, for the moment, unanswered. What is clear, however, is that a new, emerging literacy—referred to alternately as "media literacy," "information literacy," "technology literacy," or even "visual literacy"—is on the horizon. We may suppose that literature itself, while perhaps no longer constituting an essential (durable) part of what defines a literate society in the years to come, will most certainly be called upon to guide us as we reconceptualize our position in relation to knowledge at the dawn of the post-industrial information economy.

BIBLIOGRAPHY

Abbas, Ackbar. "On Fascination: Walter Benjamin's Images." *New German Critique* 48 (1989): 43–62.

Agger, Ben. *The Decline of Discourse: Reading, Writing and Resistance in Postmodern Capitalism.* London: Falmer, 1990.

Alcoff, Linda. "Cultural Feminism versus Post-Structuralism: The Identity Crisis in Feminist Theory." *Culture/Power/History.* Eds. Nicholas B. Dirks, Geoff Eley, and Sherry B. Ortner. Princeton: Princeton UP, 1994. 96–122.

Anderson, Benedict. *Imagined Communities.* London: Verso, 1983.

Antle, Martine, ed. "The Object in France Today." *Studies in Twentieth-Century Literature* 20.2 (1996).

Apter, Emily. "Fantom Images: Hervé Guibert and the Writing of 'sida' in France." *Writing AIDS: Gay Literature, Language, and Analysis.* Eds. Timothy F. Murphy and Suzanne Poirier. New York: Columbia UP, 1993. 83–97.

Aslan, Odette. "Les Paravents de Jean Genet." *Les Voies de la création théâtrale.* Eds. Denis Bablet and Jean Jacquot. Paris: CNRS, 1972. 11–107.

Augé, Marc. *Non-lieux. Introduction à une anthropologie de la surmodernité.* Paris: Seuil, 1992.

Aydintasbas, Asla. "Why they can't turn their backs on the veil." *The Independent* (London) (28 Apr. 1994): n. pag. Online. Lexis-Nexis. 4 Sept. 1998.

Bahri, Deepika. "Disembodying The Corpus: Postcolonial Pathology in Tsitsi Dangarembga's *Nervous Conditions*." *Postmodern Culture* 5.1 (1994): 1–16.

Balandier, Georges. "Images, images, images." *Cahiers Internationaux de Sociologie* 34.82 (1987): 7–22.

Barthes, Roland. *Camera Lucida.* Trans. Richard Howard. New York: Hill and Wang, 1981.

———. *A Lover's Discourse.* Trans. Richard Howard. New York: The Noonday Press, 1978.

———. *Fragments d'un discours amoureux.* Paris: Seuil, 1977.

Baudelaire, Charles. *Oeuvres complètes.* Paris: Gallimard, 1975.

Baudrillard, Jean. *Symbolic Exchange and Death.* Trans. Iain Hamilton Grant. London: Sage Publications, 1993.

———. *The Transparency of Evil*. Trans. James Benedict. London: Verso, 1993.

———. *La Transparence du mal*. Paris: Galilée, 1990.

———. Interview with Nicholas Zurbrugg. *Paragraph* 13 (1990): 285–300.

———. "Au delà du vrai et du faux ou le malin génie de l'image." *Autrement* 76 (1986): 156–162.

Bellafante, Ginia. "Feminism: It's all about me!" *Time* (29 June 1998): n. pag. Online. Internet. 30 June 1998.

Bellour, Raymond. "Une entreprise qui n'eut jamais d'exemple…" *Nottingham French Studies* 34.1 (1995): 121–130.

Benjamin, Walter. *Illuminations*. Trans. Harry Zohn. New York: Schocken Books, 1968.

Berger, John. "Un système nulle part contesté." *Manière de voir* Aug. 1995: 97.

———. *Ways of Seeing*. London: Penguin Books, 1972.

Berger, John and Jean Mohr. *Another Way of Telling*. New York: Vintage International, 1982.

Bersani, Leo. "The Gay Outlaw." *Diacritics* 24.2–3 (1994): 5–18.

Blanchot, Maurice. *The Work of Fire*. Trans. Charlotte Mandell. Stanford: Stanford UP, 1995.

———. *Michel Foucault tel que je l'imagine*. Montpellier: Fata Morgana, 1986.

———. *The Space of Literature*. Trans. Ann Smock. Lincoln: U of Nebraska P, 1982.

———. *L'Espace littéraire*. Paris: Gallimard, 1955.

Bordo, Susan. *Twilight Zones: The Hidden Life of Cultural Images from Plato to O.J.* Berkeley: U of California P, 1997.

———. *Unbearable Weight: Feminism, Western Culture, and the Body*. Berkeley: U of California P, 1993.

Boulé, Jean-Pierre. "Introduction." *Nottingham French Studies* 34.1 (1995): 1–4.

———. "Hervé Guibert à la télévision: vérité et séduction." *Nottingham French Studies* 34.1 (1995): 112–120.

Bouraoui, Nina. *L'Age blessé*. Paris: Fayard, 1998.

———. *Le Bal des murènes*. Paris: Fayard, 1996.

———. *Poing mort*. Paris: Gallimard, 1992.

———. *La Voyeuse interdite*. Paris: Gallimard, 1991.

Bradby, David. "Genet, the Theatre and the Algerian War." *Theatre Research International* 19 (1994): 226–38.

Brah, Avtar. "Re-framing Europe: En-gendered Racisms, Ethnicities and Nationalisms in Contemporary Western Europe." *Feminist Review* 45 (1993): 9–29.

Bronfen, Elisabeth. *Over her Dead Body.* New York: Routledge, 1992.

Brossard, Nicole. Interview with Lynne Huffer. *Another Look, Another Woman: Retranslations of French Feminism.* Connecticut: Yale UP, 1995. 114–118.

Buisine, Alain. "Le photographique plutôt que la photographie." *Nottingham French Studies* 34.1 (1995): 32–41.

Caron, David. "Playing Doctors: Refiguring the Doctor-Patient Relationship in Hervé Guibert's AIDS novels." *Literature and Medicine* 14.2 (1995): 237–249.

Cooper, Danielle Chavy. Rev. of *La Voyeuse interdite,* by Nina Bouraoui. *World Literature Today* 67.1 (1993): 145–146.

Darrieussecq, Marie. "La Notion du leurre chez Hervé Guibert." *Nottingham French Studies* 34.1 (1995): 82–99.

De Lauretis, Teresa, Andreas Huyssen and Kathleen Woodward, eds. *The Technological Imagination: Theories and Fictions.* Wisconsin: Coda Press, 1980.

Deleuze, Gilles. *Negotiations.* New York: Routledge, 1995.

Dort, Bernard. "Le Théâtre: Une féerie sans réplique." *Magazine Littéraire* 313 (1993): 46–50.

Duncan, Derek. "Gestes autobiographiques: le sida et les formes d'expressions artistiques du moi." *Nottingham French Studies* 34.1 (1995): 100–111.

Durham, Scott. "The Poetics of Simulation: The Simulacrum and Narrative in the Works of Jean Genet and Pierre Klossowski." Diss. Yale U, 1992.

Echnoz, Jean. *Lac.* Paris: Minuit, 1989.

Eco, Umberto. "Fourteen Ways of Looking at a Blackshirt." *New York Review of Books* (22 June, 1995): n. pag. Online. Internet. 4 Jan. 1998.

———. "Why New Media Won't Kill Books." *World Press Review* June 1996: 16–17.

———. "Afterword." *The Future of the Book.* Ed. Geoffrey Nunberg. Berkeley: U of California P, 1996. 295–306.

Edelman, Lee. "The Mirror and the Tank: 'AIDS,' Subjectivity, and the Rhetoric of Activism." *Writing AIDS: Gay Literature, Language, and Analysis.* Eds. Timothy F. Murphy and Suzanne Poirier. New York: Columbia UP, 1993: 9–38.

Finkielkraut, Alain. *La Défaite de la pensée.* Paris: Gallimard, 1987.

Fisher, Dominique. "The Blank Spaces of Interculturality." Trans. Meaghan Emery and Donna Wilkerson. *Research in African Literatures* 28.4 (1997): 85–100.

————. "'Rue du Phantasme:' Paroles et regard(s) inter-dits dans *La Voyeuse interdite* de Nina Bouraoui." *Présence francophone* 50 (1997): 45–66.

————. "Les non-lieux de Jean-Philippe Toussaint: bricol(l)age textuel et rhétorique du neutre." *University of Toronto Quarterly* 65.4 (1996): 618–631.

————. "L'abstrait et le concret d'Artaud." *Semiotica* 76.3–4 (1989): 171–89.

Flieger, Jerry Aline. "Dream, Humor and Power in Genet's *Notre-Dame-Des-Fleurs*." *French Forum* 9.1 (1984): 69–83.

Forbes, Jill and Michael Kelly, eds. *French Cultural Studies: An Introduction*. Oxford: Oxford UP, 1995.

Foucault, Michel. *The Use of Pleasure: The History of Sexuality, Vol II*. Trans. Robert Hurley. New York: Vintage, 1990.

————. "La pensée du dehors." *Critique* 229 (1964): 523–546.

Fraser, Nancy and Linda J. Nicholson. "Social Criticism without Philosophy: An Encounter between Feminism and Postmodernism." *Communication* 10.3–4 (1988): 345–366.

Fredette, Nathalie. "Jean Genet: les pouvoirs de l'imposture." *Etudes françaises* 31.3 (1995): 87–101.

Genet, Jean. *Dialogues*. Paris: Cent pages: 1990.

————. *Un Captif amoureux*. Paris: Gallimard, 1986.

————. *Les Paravents*. Lyon: L'Arbalète, 1976.

————. *Reflections on the Theatre and other writings*. Trans. Richard Seaver. London: Faber &Faber, 1972.

————. *Le Balcon*. Lyon: L'Arbalète, 1956.

————. *Pompes funèbres*. Paris: Gallimard, 1953.

————. *Querelle de Brest*. Paris: Gallimard, 1953.

————. *Notre-Dame-des-fleurs*. Lyon: L'Arbalète, 1948.

————. *Miracle de la Rose*. Lyon: L'Arbalète, 1946.

Ghafour, Hamida. "Our Culture Makes Women Define Themselves by their Looks." *The Toronto Star* (31 Jul 1998): n. pag. Online. Lexis-Nexis. 4 Sept. 1998

Gilbert, Helen. "Dressed to Kill: A Post-Colonial Reading of Costume and the Body in Australian Theatre." *Imperialism and Theatre: Essays on World Theatre,*

Drama, and Performance. Ed. J. Ellen Gainor. New York: Routledge, 1995. 105–128.

Giroud, Françoise. "Deux lions pour Fabius!" *Le Nouvel Observateur* 23–29 Jan. 1992: 31.

Giroux, Henry, et al., eds. *Counternarratives: Cultural Studies and Critical Pedagogies in Postmodern Spaces.* New York: Routledge, 1996.

———. "Slacking Off: Border Youth and Postmodern Culture." *Counternarratives: Cultural Studies and Critical Pedagogies in Postmodern Spaces.* New York: Routledge, 1996: 59–80.

Gregg, John. *Maurice Blanchot and the Literature of Transgression.* Princeton: Princeton UP, 1994.

Grenier, Richard. "Fascism à la Française." *National Review* 49.23 (1997): 46–50.

Guibert, Hervé. *La Pîqure d'amour et autres textes,* suivi de *La Chair fraîche.* Paris: Gallimard, 1994.

———. *L'Homme au chapeau rouge.* Paris: Gallimard, 1992.

———. *Mon Valet et moi.* Paris: Seuil, 1991.

———. *Le Protocole compassionnel.* Paris: Gallimard, 1991.

———. *A l'ami qui ne m'a pas sauvé la vie.* Paris: Gallimard, 1990.

———. *L'Incognito.* Paris: Gallimard, 1989.

———. *Mauve le vierge.* Paris: Gallimard, 1988.

———. *L'Image fantôme.* Paris: Minuit, 1982.

Guillaume, Marc. "Le Carnaval des spectres." *Cahiers Internationaux de Sociologie.* 34.82 (1987): 73–81.

Harris, Frederick. "Linguistic Reality—Historical Reality: Genet, Céline, Grass." *Neohelicon* 14.2 (1987): 257–273.

Heath, Stephen. "Friday Night Books." *A New History of French Literature.* Ed. Denis Hollier. Cambridge: Harvard UP, 1989. 1054–1062.

Hebdige, Dick. "After the Masses." *Culture/Power/History.* Eds. Nicholas B. Dirks, Geoff Eley, and Sherry B. Ortner. Princeton: Princeton UP, 1994. 222–235.

Henric, Jacques. "Le Saint Suaire ou la puissance du négatif." *Autrement* 76 (1986): 184–89.

Hooks, bell. *Teaching to Transgress.* New York: Routledge, 1994.

Hutcheon, Linda. *The Politics of Postmodernism.* London: Routledge, 1989.

Huyssen, Andreas. *Twilight Memories.* London: Routledge, 1995.

————. *After the Great Divide: Modernism, Mass Culture, Postmodernism.* Bloomington: Indiana UP, 1986.

Katzman, Melanie A. and Sing Lee. "Beyond Body Image: the Integration of Feminist and Transcultural Theories in the Understanding of Self Starvation." *The International Journal of Eating Disorders* 22.4 (1997): 385–394.

Kirkup, James. "Obituary: Hervé Guibert." *The Independent* (21 Jan. 1992): n. pag. Online. Lexis-Nexis. 15 Mar. 1998.

Korac, Maja. "Serbian Nationalism: Nationalism of My Own People." *Feminist Review* 45 (1993): 108–112.

Lankshear, Colin, Michael Peters and Michele Knobel. "Critical Pedagogy and Cyberspace." *Counternarratives: Cultural Studies and Critical Pedagogies in Postmodern Spaces.* Eds. Henry Giroux et al. New York: Routledge, 1996. 49–188.

Leclerc, Yvan. "Autour de Minuit." *Dalhousie French Studies* 17 (1989): 63–74.

Mantovani, Giuseppe. "Virtual Reality as a Communication Environment: Consensual Hallucination, Fiction, and Possible Selves." *Human Relations* 48.6(1995): 669–84.

McHale, Brian. *Postmodernist Fiction.* London: Routledge, 1987.

McLaren, Peter and Rhonda Hammer. "Media Knowledges, Warrior Citizenry, and Postmodern Literacies." *Counternarratives: Cultural Studies and Critical Pedagogies in Postmodern Spaces.* New York: Routledge, 1996. 81–116.

McLuhan, Marshall. *On McLuhan: Forward Through the Rearview Mirror.* Eds. Paul Benedetti and Nancy DeHart. Scarborough: Prentice-Hall Canada, 1996.

Michaud, Ginette. "Récits postmodernes?" *Etudes françaises* 21.3 (1985–1986): 67–88.

"MWL chief addresses letter to Mongella; UN Conference on Women in Beijing." *Saudi Gazette* (1 Sept. 1995): n. pag. Online. Lexis-Nexis. 4 Sept. 1998.

Nericcio, William. "Artif[r]acture: Virulent Pictures, Graphic Narrative and the Ideology of the Visual." *Mosaic* 28.4 (1995): 79–101.

Okin, Susan Moller. "Feminism and Multiculturalism: Some Tensions." *Ethics* 108.4 (1998): 661–685.

Oswald, Laura. "Middle East Voices." *Diacritics* 21.1 (1991): 46–62.

————. *Jean Genet and the Semiotics of Performance.* Bloomington: Indiana UP, 1989.

Paz, Octavio. "The Cathedral of Literature." *New Perspectives Quarterly* 11.3 (1994): 1.

Pfeil, Fred. *Another Tale to Tell: Politics and Narrative in Postmodern Culture*. London: Verso, 1990.

Plunka, Gene. *The Rites of Passage of Jean Genet: The Art and the Aesthetics of Risk Taking*. London: Fairleigh Dickinson UP, 1992.

Pollock, Griselda, *Vision & Difference. Femininity, Feminism and the Histories of Art*. New York: Routledge, 1988.

Pratt, Murray. "*Hôtel Old Cataract*: Image, texte." *Nottingham French Studies* 34.1 (1995): 5–7.

———. "De la Désidentification à l'Incognito: A la recherche d'une autobiographique homosexuelle." *Nottingham French Studies* 34.1 (1995): 70–81.

Raz, Aviad E. and Rina Shapira. "A Symbolic Interactionist User's Guide to the Answering Machine: 22 Reflections on Vocal Encounters in an Emerging Social World." *Symbolic Interaction* 17.4 (1994): 411–429.

Rambali, Paul. "Bitter Cry from the Confessional." *The Guardian* (London) 23 Jan. 1992: 22.

Rich, Adrienne. "Compulsory Heterosexuality and Lesbian Existence." *Blood, Bread, and Poetry*. New York: W.W. Norton & Company, 1986. 23–75.

———. *Of Woman Born*. Tenth Anniversary Edition. New York: W.W. Norton & Company, 1986.

Robins, Kevin. *Into the Image: Culture and Politics in the Field of Vision*. London: Routledge, 1996.

Said, Edward. "The Reith Lectures: Speaking Truth to Power." *The Independent* (London) 22 Jul. 1993: Feature Page 12.

Sartre, Jean-Paul. *Saint Genet: Actor and Martyr*. Trans. Bernard Frechtman. London: Heinemann, 1963.

Schehr, Lawrence. "Hervé Guibert under Bureaucratic Quarantine." *L'Esprit créateur* 34.1 (1994): 73–82.

Sherzer, Dina. "Effets d'intertextualité dans *Shérazade* et *Les Carnets de Shérazade* de Leïla Sebbar." *Regards sur la France des années 1980: le Roman*. Eds. Joseph Brami, Madeleine Cottenet-Hague, and Pierre Verdaguen. Saratoga: Anma Libri, 1994. 21–31.

Shaviro, Steven. *The Cinematic Body*. Minnesota: U. of Minnesota P, 1993.

Shohat, Ella and Robert Stam. *Unthinking Eurocentrism*. London: Routledge, 1994.

Silverstone, Roger. "Let us Return to the Murmuring of Everyday Practices: A Note on Michel de Certeau, Television, and Everyday Life." *Theory, Culture, & Society* 6 (1989): 77–94.

Simons, Jon. *Foucault & the political.* London: Routledge, 1995.

Simons, Marlise. "Cry of Muslim Women for Equal Rights is Rising." *New York Times* 9 Mar. 1998, late ed.: A1[+].

Smyth, Edmund. "Des aveugles: Modes d'articulation." *Nottingham French Studies* 34.1 (1995): 8–14.

Sontag, Susan. *AIDS and its Metaphors.* New York: Farrar Straus Giroux, 1989.

———. *Under the Sign of Saturn.* New York: Noonday Press, 1980.

Sorlin, Pierre. *Mass Media.* London: Routledge, 1994.

Storzer, Gerald H. "The Homosexual Paradigm in Balzac, Gide and Genet." *Homosexualities in French Literature.* Eds. George Stambolian and Elaine Marks. London: Cornell UP, 1979. 186–209.

Talens, Jenaro. "Writing against Simulacrum: The Place of Literature and Literary Theory in the Electronic Age." *Boundary 2* 22.1 (1995): 1–21.

Taylor, Mark and Esa Saarinen. *Imagologies: Media Philosophy.* London: Routledge, 1994.

Thompson, William, ed. *The Contemporary Novel in France.* Gainesville: U of Florida P, 1995.

Tomlinson, John. *Cultural Imperialism.* Baltimore: John Hopkins UP, 1991.

Traube, Elizabeth. "Secrets of Success in Postmodern Society." *Culture/Power/History.* Eds. Nicholas B. Dirks, Geoff Eley, and Sherry B. Ortner. Princeton: Princeton UP, 1994. 557–584.

Treadway, Joan. "Muslim Women Fight Stereotypes." *The Plain Dealer* 21 Jul. 1998: Everywoman section, 6F.

Turkle, Sherry. "Constructions and Reconstructions of Self in Virtual Reality: Playing in the MUDs." *Mind, Culture, and Activity* 1.3 (1994): 158–167.

Ubersfeld, Anne. "Kantor ou La Parole de la mort." *La Mort dans le texte.* Ed. Gilles Ernst. Lyon: Presses Universitaires de Lyon, 1988. 245–63.

Vaget, Hans Rudolf. "Confession and Camouflage: The Diaries of Thomas Mann." *The Journal of English and Germanic Philology* 96.4 (1997): 567–591.

Walker, David. "Antecedents for Genet's Persona." *Autobiography and the Existential Self.* Eds. T. Keefe and E. Smyth. Liverpool: Liverpool UP, 1994. 147–168.

Watts, Philip. "Political Discourse and Poetic Register in Jean Genet's *Pompes funèbres.*" *French Forum* 17.2 (1992): 191–203.

Weinel, Eleanor. "Ashes to Ashes, Dust to Dust: Is there any future for cemeteries?" *USA Today* Jan 1996: 49–50.

Williamson, Judith. "Woman Is an Island: Femininity and Colonization." *Studies in Entertainment: Critical Approaches to Mass Culture.* Ed. Tania Modleski. Bloomington: Indiana UP, 1986.

Yusufali, Sultana. "My body is my own business." *The Toronto Star* 17 Feb. 1998: Section Life, Young Street, C1.

Yuval-Davis, Nira. "Ethnicity, Gender Relations and Multiculturalism." *Debating Cultural Hybridity.* Eds. Pnina Werbner and Tariq Modood. London: Zed Books, 1997: 193–208.